SIMPLIFIED GRAMMAR OF THE TELUGU LANGUAGE

BY

HENRY MORRIS

GYAN

Published by

Gyan Publishing House
5, Ansari Road
Daryaganj, New Delhi-110002
Phone: 011-47034999, 9811692060
E-mail: books@gyanbooks.com

Distribution Network
gyanbooks.com
India, USA, Canada, UK, Australia

ISBN: 978-93-6433-846-2 (HB)
First Published, 1890

2nd Impression 2024

Printed at: Gyan Press, Delhi.

SIMPLIFIED GRAMMAR OF THE TELUGU LANGUAGE
Author: HENRY MORRIS

SIMPLIFIED GRAMMAR

OF THE

TELUGU LANGUAGE.

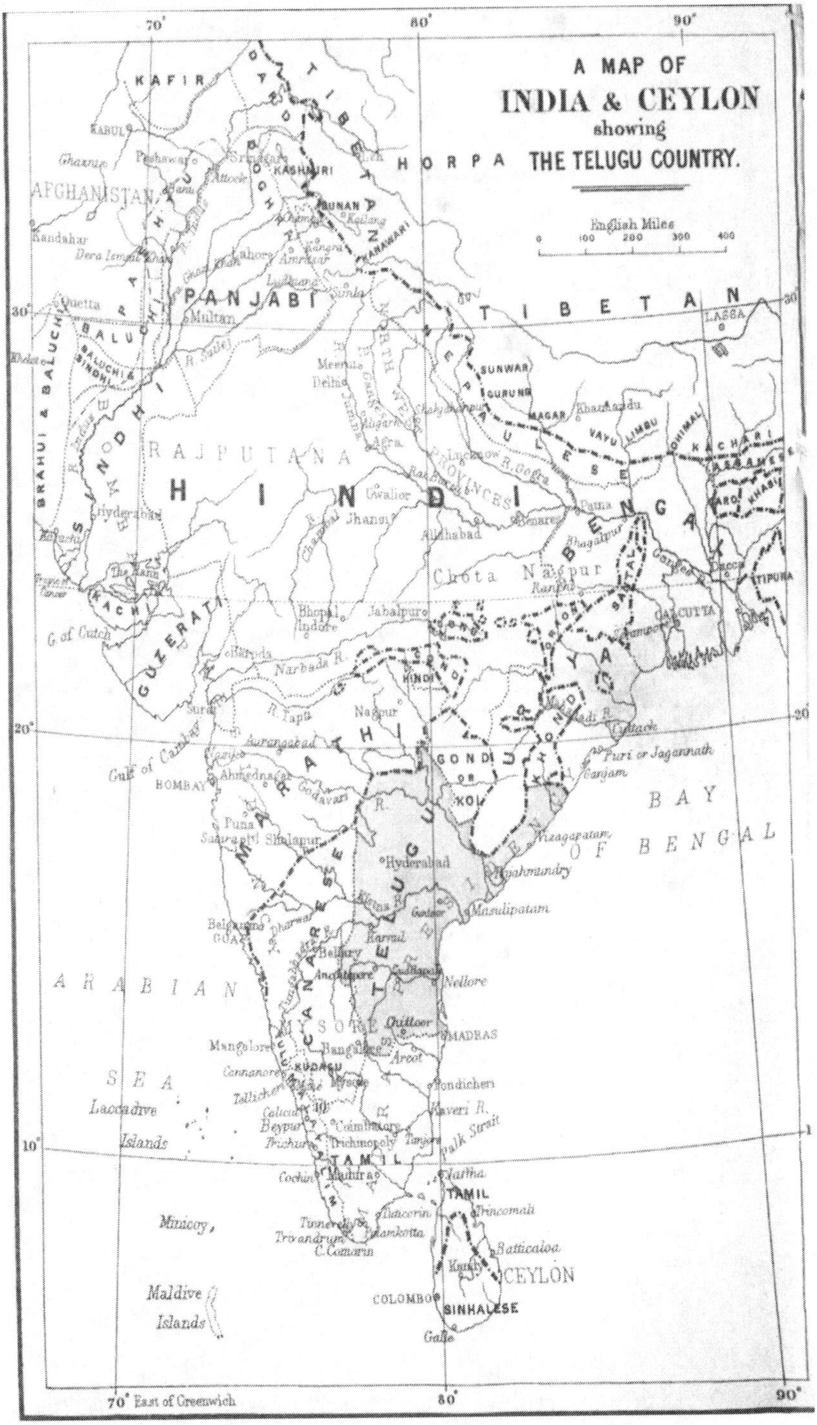

A MAP OF
INDIA & CEYLON
showing
THE TELUGU COUNTRY.
English Miles
0 100 200 300 400
70°
80°
90°
30°
20°
10°
70° East of Greenwich
KAFIR
HORPA
TIBETAN
PANJABI
RAJPUTANA
HINDI
BENGALI
AFGHANISTAN
KASHMIRI
BRAHUI & BALUCHI
SINDHI
GUZERATI
MARATHI
TELUGU
CANARESE
MYSORE
TAMIL
SINHALESE
CEYLON
GOND
KOL
ARABIAN SEA
BAY OF BENGAL
Laccadive Islands
Maldive Islands
Minicoy
Kabul
Kandahar
Peshawar
Lahore
Multan
Quetta
Simla
Delhi
Agra
Gwalior
Jhansi
Allahabad
Benares
Patna
Chota Nagpur
Jabalpur
Bhopal
Indore
Nagpur
Narbada R.
Surat
Aurangabad
BOMBAY
Ahmednagar
Puna
Hyderabad
Kistna R.
Guntur
Masulipatam
Rajahmundry
Vizagapatam
Ganjam
Puri or Jagannath
Cuttack
CALCUTTA
Bellary
Nellore
Chittoor
MADRAS
Bangalore
Arcot
Mangalore
Cannanore
Pondicheri
Calicut
Coimbatore
Trichinopoly
Tanjore
Palk Strait
Cochin
Madura
Tinnevelly
Palamkotta
Trevandrum
C. Comorin
Trincomali
Batticaloa
Kandy
COLOMBO
Galle
LASSA
Khatmandu
TIPURA

SIMPLIFIED GRAMMAR

OF THE

TELUGU LANGUAGE

BY

HENRY MORRIS, M.R.A.S., F.R.G.S.

Madras Civil Service (retired)

AUTHOR OF A SCHOOL "HISTORY OF INDIA," "HISTORY OF THE GODAVERY DISTRICT" AND OTHER WORKS

WITH A MAP OF INDIA SHOWING THE TELUGU COUNTRY

LONDON

KEGAN PAUL, TRENCH, TRÜBNER & CO., LTD.

1890

PREFACE.

JUST a few words may be considered necessary regarding the plan of the following brief Grammar. I have carefully read the late Professor Palmer's original Prospectus to this Series of Simplified Grammars, and have endeavoured faithfully to carry out his idea. I have diligently examined the structure of the Telugu language, and have tried to show how, to a considerable extent, what appear to us irregularities and peculiarities are merely euphonic changes which, in course of time, have become integral portions of the tongue. I have, however, endeavoured to make the work, as a whole, consistent and self-contained; and, with this purpose, I have thought it right to give a longer account of the verbs, and especially of the auxiliary verbs, than Professor Palmer intended, and I have given a tolerably full paradigm of a verb in all its parts, as I did not consider the grammar complete without it.

I have written as plainly and simply as I can, and have used only such forms as are generally employed in daily life and conversation, so as to make the book both concise and practical. Its very simplicity has been my greatest difficulty. I shall be amply rewarded if this little volume should prove of some service to beginners in acquiring the knowledge of one of the sweetest languages of the East.

HENRY MORRIS.

BLACKHEATH, *October*, 1890

TABLE OF CONTENTS.

IV. Syntax.

SIMPLIFIED TELUGU GRAMMAR.

SIMPLIFIED TELUGU GRAMMAR.

I. INTRODUCTION.

1. Telugu is one of the four great Dravidian languages spoken in South India. It is not a mere dialect of the same language as the Tamilians and the other inhabitants of the south formerly spoke; but a distinct and separate language, though of the same family. That the people dwelling in the Telugu country were a civilized, though a simple and pastoral, race, is proved by the fact that every requirement of men gathered together in a well organized society can be expressed in pure Telugu without the assistance of the more stately language of the Áryan invader. The stock-words, or those used in the intercourse of everyday life, are of old Dravidian origin; but the language has been strengthened and enriched by additions from Sanskrit, as English has been by Latin and Greek. The original words are short and simple. They are seldom more than two syllables in length; and, as the genius of the language demands, every word properly ends in a vowel. The best Telugu consists of such words skilfully mingled with a few Sanskrit derivatives, just as the best and most nervous English is that in which plain Saxon words are used with the least admixture of Latin.

2. Telugu is singularly melodious. It is the sweetest and most musical of all the Dravidian tongues, and it sounds harmonious even on the lips of the most illiterate.

It has justly been called the Italian of the East; and though Tamil may, perhaps, be a richer language, and more wealthy in classical literature, Telugu confessedly bears the palm for its exquisite melody and grace.

3. Telugu is spoken in the northern part of the Presidency of Madras. As the people speaking it are scattered over a wide territory, which is partly within the British dominions and partly without, it is difficult to ascertain its exact area, but it is estimated at about one hundred thousand square miles. It includes the districts of Vizagapatam, the Godavari, the Kistna, Nellore, Cuddapah, Kurnool, and parts of Ganjam, Bellary, Anantapore, and North Arcot, together with the eastern portions of the dominions of the Nizam and the Maharajah of Mysore. The number of the Telugu-speaking people is estimated at 11,610,000 according to the census of 1881; but it must be borne in mind that there are very many whose native language is Telugu now living in the Tamil and Canarese countries.

4. The Telugu character is written, as in all the Dravidian languages that have been reduced to writing, from left to right. It is rounded and full of circles. In the common written character the syllables and words are usually linked together, and it should be remembered that, unlike English, the letters should be made to slope a little towards the left. It is generally the custom now to print the words separately, but this is distinctly adopted from the European custom.

5. In reading and speaking, every letter should be pro-

nounced. Great care should be taken that, when consonants are doubled, both should be clearly enunciated, and much nicety and discrimination are required in distinguishing between the soft and the hard consonants, and in pronouncing the aspirate, which, as a rule, is always inherent in the aspirated consonants. Those who reside in the country will find it a great help never, at first, to pronounce a word without hearing it correctly pronounced by the lips of a Telugu man. In the initial stages of study, the ear should take the precedence of the eye, the tongue, and the hand. In other words, reading, speaking, and writing should, at first, give way to listening. The correct pronunciation of the different *t's* and *d's* at the commencement is simply invaluable. If this is carefully attended to, Telugu will be found, in comparison with many other Oriental languages, exceedingly easy.

6. Telugu is an agglutinative language, that is, the particles used to form the termination of words are affixed or 'glued on' to the words which they modify.

II. ORTHOGRAPHY.

(1.) VOWELS.

1. The vowels have two forms—the initial and the medial.

2. The initial form is used only at the beginning of a word, and the medial form is employed when it is joined to a consonant.

3. The following are the initial forms of the vowels. They go in pairs, the long vowels being twice the length of the short in pronunciation.

Telugu form.	*Transliteration.*	*English sound.*
అ	*a*	Americ*a*.
ఆ	*á*	F*a*r.
ఇ or యి	*i*	P*i*n.
ఈ or యీ	*í*	Mach*i*ne.
ఉ or వు	*u*	P*u*ll.
ఊ or వూ	*ú*	R*u*le.
ఎ or యె	*e*	L*e*t.
ఏ or యే	*é*	Th*e*re.
ఒ or వొ	*o*	P*o*lice.
ఓ or వో	*ó*	St*o*ne.

The vowels *i* and *í* are, sometimes in print and almost invariably in writing, represented by యి and యీ. In the same manner, *e* and *é* are preceded by *y*, the Telugu-speaking people pronouncing even English words beginning with these vowels with an initial *y*. In ordinary writing *u* and *ú* *o* and *ó* are written with a *v* preceding them. Thus: *vu* and *vú*, *vo* and *vó*; but the *v* is not pronounced. It must be particularly remembered that these vowels never have the soft sound which they have in English, as in the word '*u*se.'

4. The short, clipped sounds of *a* and *o*, as in the English words '*can*' and '*con*' are not represented in

Telugu, and great care should be taken never to pronounce these vowels thus, when speaking Telugu.

5. There are also the semi-vowels ఋ *ru* and ౠ *rú* and ఌ *lu*, which are not in common use.

6. There are also the two diphthongs

ఐ	*ai*	*Ai*sle.
ఔ	*au*	P*ou*t.

The former is generally written అయి *ai*, and the latter అవు *avu*, the *v*, in this case, not being pronounced.

(2.) (*a*) CONSONANTS.

7. The greater number of the consonants require the medial vowel mark, as they cannot be pronounced without the vowel sound; and, therefore, it is proposed to give them, in the first instance, with the medial sign and the sound of the first vowel, *a*. The mode of connecting the other vowels will then be explained.

8. అ *a* in its medial form takes the simple shape of a curved line, either attached to the top of the letter or placed closed to it without touching it.

Telugu.	*Transliteration.*	*English.*
క	*ka*	*K*ing.
ఖ	*kha*	In*k*-*h*orn.
గ	*ga*	*G*ive.
ఘ	*gha*	Sta*g*-*h*orn.

Telugu.	*Transliteration.*	*English.*
ఙ	*gnya*	Onion.
చ	*cha, tsa*	*Ch*ase, *Ts*ar.
ఛ	*chha, tsha*	Coa*ch-h*ouse.
జ	*ja, za*	*J*ar, a*dz*e.
ఝ	*jha*	He*dge-h*og.
ఞ	*nya*	Mi*gn*onette.
ట	*ṭa*	*T*artar.
ఠ	*ṭha*	Car*t-h*orse.
డ	*ḍa*	*D*rum.
ఢ	*ḍha*	Bi*d h*im.
ణ	*ṇa*	*N*o.
త	*ta*	*T*ube.
థ	*tha*	No*t h*ere.
ద	*da*	*D*upe.
ధ	*dha*	A*dh*ere.
న	*na*	*N*ag.
ప	*pa*	*P*ar.
ఫ	*pha*	U*p h*ere.
బ	*ba*	*B*ird.
భ	*bha*	Clu*b-h*ouse.
మ	*ma*	*M*ap.
య	*ya*	Yard.
ర	*ra*	*R*ag.

Telugu.	*Transliteration.*	*English.*
ల	*la*	*L*ad.
వ	*va*	*V*at.
శ	*ṣa*	*Sh*arp.
ష	*sha*	Pu*sh*.
స	*sa*	*S*alt.
హ	*ha*	*H*ale.
ళ	*ḷa*	C*l*erk.
క్ష	*ksha*	Kic*ksh*aw.

There are also the signs ం, which is pronounced *m* or *n* according to the letter that succeeds it, and ః *ah*, the final aspirate with which some syllables and words are closed.

9. It will be observed that some of the above consonants have no vowel mark at all, and that the six consonants ఘ *gha*, ప *pa*, ఫ *pha*, ష *sha*, స *sa*, and హ *ha* have the vowel mark written unattached. In fact, the only difference between ప and వ *pa* and *va*, and between స and న *sa* and *na*, is in the connection or disconnection of the vowel mark from the body of the letter.

10. The following table of the consonants arranged in order according to their mode of pronunciation, is given, not only for the convenience of those who are acquainted with Sanskrit, but also to show at a glance the consonants which, as will be described hereafter, are mutually interchangeable.

	Hard Consonants.		Soft Consonants.		Corresponding Nasals.	Corresponding Sibilants.	Semi-vowels.
Gutturals...	క *ka*	ఖ *kha*	గ *ga*	ఘ *gha*	ఙ *ṅya*		హ *ha*
Palatals ...	చ *cha*	ఛ *chha*	జ *ja*	ఝ *jha*	ఞ	శ *ṣa*	య *ya*
Cerebrals...	ట *ṭa*	ఠ *ṭha*	డ *ḍa*	ఢ *ḍha*	ణ *ṇa*	ష *sha*	ర *ra*
							ళ *ḷa*
Dentals ...	త *ta*	థ *tha*	ద *da*	ధ *dha*	న *na*	స *sa*	ల *la*
Labials ...	ప *pa*	ఫ *pha*	బ *ba*	భ *bha*	మ *ma*		వ *va*

11. Few of the consonants require any remarks, as most of them are pronounced exactly like their English equivalents; but some explanatory observations are needed regarding those few. It will at once be noticed that there are more *t*'s and *d*'s than in English, and no English sound exactly corresponds to any of them, the soft letters being a little softer, and the hard letters a little harsher than the English. Great pains should be taken to acquire the correct pronunciation of each of these letters, for many words are spelt and pronounced in what is apparently a similar manner, the soft or the hard *t* or *d* being the only distinction between them, and the wrong pronunciation may make a vast difference in the meaning. Thus one may intend to ask for గుడ్డు *guḍḍu*, an egg, and he may really demand గుద్దు *guddu*, a blow.

12. త *ta* and ద *da* are soft, dental letters, and should be pronounced with the tongue touching the teeth, whereas

ట *ta* and డ *ḍa* are hard, cerebral letters, and should be pronounced with the tongue touching the palate, thus imparting a stronger and firmer tone to the sound.

13. న *na*, ల *la*, and స *sa* are comparatively soft; but ణ *ṇa*, ళ *ḷa*, and ష *ṣa* should be pronounced in a harder and harsher manner, like the cerebral *ṭ* and *ḍ*. వ is sometimes pronounced *wa*, especially when in combination with other consonants.

14. చ and జ have both the hard sounds *cha* and *ja*, and also the soft sounds *tsa* and *za*. The latter sounds are peculiar to pure Dravidian words, and the former principally occur in Sanskrit and other foreign and imported words. These two letters, as a rule, take the harder sound before the vowels *i*, *í* and *e*, *é* and the diphthong *ai*, and the softer when followed by the other vowels. Thus: చెయ్యి *cheyy*, the hand, చోటు *tsóṭu*, a place; జలము *jalamu*, water, రాజు *rázu*, a king.

15. The nasal letter ఞ *nya* is never used alone. It is always supported by జ *j*, under which it is written, and the double letter is pronounced *gnya*. Thus: ఆజ్ఞ *ágnya*, a command.

16. When the letter ర *ra* is used before another consonant, it has sometimes a second form, namely, ౯, which is written after the succeeding consonant. Thus: కర్త *karta*, a lord. There is another form of *r*, which sometimes occurs in books; but it is practically obsolete in the ordi-

nary written character. This form is ఱ. *R* should always be clearly pronounced, and never slurred over, as is frequently the case in English. Thus, in the above mentioned word కర్త *karta,* the *r* should be plainly enunciated, as it would be by a Scotchman.

17. The letter న *na* also has a second form, namely న్ when it is intended to be final, and the speaker irregularly clips his words. Thus, in వచ్చెను *vachchenu,* he came, if the *u* is dropped, the final *n* becomes వచ్చెన్ *vachchen.*

18. When the sign *sunna* or ం is used, it is pronounced *n* before the letters up to న *na;* but before the remaining consonants and at the end of words, it is pronounced *m.* Thus: in వంక *vanka,* crooked, it is pronounced *n,* but in సంశయం *samṣayam,* doubt, it is in both places pronounced *m.*

19. It may here be stated that, although every word in the language properly ends in a vowel, words ending in ము *mu* are almost invariably, though irregularly, pronounced in common conversation as if they ended in *m.* Thus: hardly any one says గుర్రము *gurramu,* a horse, in full, but *gurram,* though the first pronunciation is correct, and the latter is not. The full grammatical expression, as is so frequently the case in English, sounds pedantic.

20. The letter హ *ha,* when it immediately precedes another consonant, is pronounced after it, the Telugu language not allowing so harsh a sound as would be produced by attempting to pronounce it before the succeeding

consonant. The aspirate should be clearly enunciated. Thus: బ్రాహ్మణుడు *Brámhaṇuḍu,* a Brahmin.

21. The sign ః is used as a silent aspirate, or as an *h* not succeeded by a vowel, and is pronounced as a soft breathing after the consonant that follows it. It is most frequently used in Sanskrit words. Thus: దుఃఖము *dukhhamu,* sorrow.

22. For the sake of convenience the consonants have hitherto been represented in combination with the vowel *a,* not only to give life or breath to the consonants; but also because those consonants which need the affixing of a vowel mark would look awkward and ungainly without one. The medial forms of the other vowels, omitting the very uncommon ones, will now be described. Each consonant will be given in turn.

23. The medial form of ఆ *á* is represented by a long stroke, written from left to right, with a small circle at the end, thus, ా.

కా	ఖా	గా	ఘా	చా	ఛా	జా	ఝా	టా	ఠా
ká	*khá*	*gá*	*ghá*	*chá*	*chhá*	*já*	*jhá*	*ṭá*	*ṭhá*

డా	ఢా	ణా	తా	థా	దా	ధా	నా	పా	ఫా	బా
ḍá	*ḍha*	*ṇá*	*tá*	*thá*	*dá*	*dhá*	*ná*	*pá*	*phá*	*bá*

భా	మా	యా	రా	లా	వా	శా	షా	సా	హా	ళా	క్షా
bhá	*má*	*yá*	*rá*	*lá*	*vá*	*ṣá*	*shá*	*sá*	*há*	*ḷá*	*kshá*

24. The medial forms of *i* and *í* are a little semicircle in the former instance, and the long vowel is represented by a little flourish above the semicircle.

Thus: కి కీ ఖి ఖీ గి గీ చి చీ జి జీ టి టీ
ki kí khi khí gi gí chi chí ji jí ṭi ṭí

డి డీ ణి ణీ తి తీ ది దీ ధి ధీ ని నీ పి పీ
ḍi ḍí ṇi ṇí ti tí di dí dhi dhí ni ní pi pí

బి బీ మి మీ యి యీ రి రీ లి లీ వి వీ శి శీ
bi bí mi mí yi yí ri rí li lí vi ví ṣi ṣí

షి షీ సి సీ హి హీ ళి ళీ క్షి క్షీ
shi shí si sí hi hí ḷi ḷí kshi kshí

It will be observed that, as in the case of the first vowel, these medial signs are not affixed to the letters to the consonants పి *pi* ఫి *phi*, షి *shi*, సి *si*, and హి *hi*, but are written close to the side of the consonant; and that ఖి *khi*, జి *ji*, టి *ṭi*, ణి *ṇi*, బి *bi*, and లి *li*, which do not take the sign *a*, have these and the other vowel marks attached to them. The long vowel in మీ *mí* and యీ is represented by the long form of ఆ *á* being attached to their right side, instead of by the flourish at the top.

25. *U* and *ú* are represented by an open semicircle being placed on the right side of the consonant, the sign of the long *á* being affixed to the semicircle to lengthen the *u*.

Thus: కు కూ గు గూ చు చూ జు జూ టు టూ
ku kú gu gú tsu tsú zu zú ṭu ṭú

డు డూ ణు ణూ తు తూ దు దూ ను నూ పు పూ
ḍu ḍú ṇu ṇú tu tú du dú nu nú pu pú

బు బూ ము మూ యు యూ రు రూ లు లూ వు వూ
bu bú mu mú yu yú ru rú lu lú vu vú

శు శూ షు షూ సు సూ హు హూ ళు ళూ
ṣu ṣú shu shú su sú hu hú ḷu ḷú

26. It will be observed that, while, in some of these forms, the sign of the vowel *a* is displaced by the medial marks of *u* and *ú*, it is retained in most cases, and the other forms are used in addition to it. Thus, in కు *ku*, కూ *kú*, గు *gu*, గూ *gú*, and ము *mu* మూ *mú*, the sign of *a* is retained, and the signs of *u* and *ú* are added at the side of the consonants.

27. Attention is also drawn to the fact that the signs of these vowels are joined to the letters ప *pa*, ఫ *pha*, and వ *va* in a different manner than to the other consonants, being placed under these letters instead of at their side, in order to distinguish them from ఘ *gha* and మ *ma*. Thus: పువ్వు *puvvu*, a flower.

28. The vowel *e* is represented in the medial form by ె, written from right to left, it being lengthened by a flourish on the top. Thus:

కె	కే	గె	గే	చె	చే	జె	జే	టె	టే	డె	డే	తె	తే
ke	*ké*	*ge*	*gé*	*che*	*ché*	*je*	*jé*	*ṭe*	*ṭé*	*ḍe*	*ḍé*	*te*	*té*
దె	దే	నె	నే	పె	పే	బె	బే	మె	మే	యె	యే		
de	*dé*	*ne*	*né*	*pe*	*pé*	*be*	*bé*	*me*	*mé*	*ye*	*yé*		
రె	రే	లె	లే	వె	వే	శె	శే	షె	షే	సె	సే		
re	*ré*	*le*	*lé*	*ve*	*vé*	*ṣe*	*ṣé*	*she*	*shé*	*se*	*sé*		
హె	హే	ళె	ళే										
he	*hé*	*ḷe*	*ḷé*										

29. The vowels *o* and *ó* are represented in their medial form by a curved line with a slight dip in the centre and a circle at the end, the long vowel being indicated by the

circle being continued above and made into a flourish. Thus:

కొ	కో	గొ	గో	చొ	చో	జొ	జో	టొ	టో	డొ	డో
ko	*kó*	*go*	*gó*	*tso*	*tsó*	*zo*	*zó*	*ṭo*	*ṭó*	*ḍo*	*ḍó*
తొ	తో	దొ	దో	పొ	పో	బొ	బో	రొ	రో	లొ	లో
to	*tó*	*do*	*dó*	*po*	*pó*	*bo*	*bó*	*ro*	*ró*	*lo*	*ló*
షొ	షో	శొ	శో	సొ	సో	ళొ	ళో				
ṣo	*ṣó*	*sho*	*shó*	*so*	*só*	*ḷo*	*ḷó*				

30. It should be remembered that, in writing this sign in connection with the letters పొ *po* and సొ *so*, the dent in the curved line must always be placed to the left of the consonant.

31. These vowels are also represented by the sign of the vowel *e* being used together with the sign of *u* or *ú* placed to the right of the consonant. This is always the case with the consonants న *na*, మ *ma*, య *ya*, and వ *va*; but these signs are frequently used in manuscript with other letters also. This arises from the sounds *e* and *u* in combination becoming *o*.

Thus:	నొ	నో	మొ	మో	యొ	యో	వొ	వో
	no	*nó*	*mo*	*mó*	*yo*	*yó*	*vo*	*vó*

It will be observed that the signs in మో *mó* and యో *yó* are written in a contracted form, *e* and *á* being substituted for *e* and *ú*.

32. The diphthongs *ai* and *au* are used in their medial forms as follows:

కై గై చై జై టై డై తై దై నై పై
kai gai chai jai ṭai ḍai tai dai nai pai

బై మై యై రై లై వై సై ళై కౌ గౌ చౌ
bai mai yai rai lai vai sai ḷai kau gau chau

జౌ టౌ డౌ తౌ దౌ నౌ పౌ బౌ మౌ యౌ
jau ṭau ḍau tau dau nau pau bau mau yau

రౌ లౌ వౌ సౌ ళౌ
rau lau vau sau ḷau

These rows of combined letters may at first sight appear intricate and perplexing; but a little perseverance will enable any one to master them in a very short time. The principle of the formation of each medial vowel is the same throughout, with really very few and slight variations, and it is not difficult in application to the several letters. It is strongly recommended that the student, if in India, should, at first, patiently write the letters from set copies, and continue the practice for some time until he has thoroughly acquired the habit of accurate and ready writing.

(b.) Double Form of the Consonants.

33. When consonants are doubled, the second letter is placed under the first, but without the vowel mark being attached to it. In most cases this second consonant takes its own proper shape; but the eight following consonants have another and an entirely different form—namely, క *ka*, త *ta*, న *na*, మ *ma*, య *ya*, ర *ra*, ల *la*, and వ *va*. The second form of these consonants are as follows: క్క *kka*, త్త *tta*, న్న *nna*, మ్మ *mma*, య్య *yya*, ర్ర *rra*, ల్ల *lla*, and వ్వ *vva*. The

second form of a consonant can, in a similar manner, be affixed to any other consonant. Thus: త్క *tka,* డ్ల *ḍla,* వ్ర *vra.* Both letters should be clearly pronounced. Three consonants can also be similarly combined, the second form of the two latter being employed. Thus: క్త్వ *ktwa,* డ్ర్య *ḍrya.*

34. As a rule, the vowel marks are attached to the first of the doubled consonants; but, when పు *pu* or పూ *pú* is doubled, the vowel mark is attached to the second consonant. Thus: in నిప్పు *nippu,* fire, it will be observed that the vowel form is attached to the second *p,* but at the side of it, and not underneath.

35. The second form of గ *ga,* namely, గ్గ *gga,* appears to be different from the first; but it is really the same, because the lower portion of గ *ga* is usually written like a semicircle.

36. There are certain peculiarities in pronunciation, which are very common, but can only be thoroughly learned by constant practice in talking. Thus: చేప *chépa,* a fish, చేత *chéta,* by or in the hand, are almost invariably, though ungrammatically, pronounced *chyápa* and *chyáta.*

(3.) Euphony in Pronunciation.

37. Telugu, the sweetest of Oriental languages, is peculiarly sensitive to anything like an hiatus in speech. As each word ends in a vowel, it is necessary, when any word in

a sentence precedes another which commences with a vowel, to use some device for preventing the hiatus in sound. Either the first vowel is dropped altogether, and the two words run into each other, or a soft and liquid consonant is inserted between them, in order to ensure euphony in the pronunciation. Thus: when the two words రమ్ము *rammu*, come, and అను *anu*, tell (him), are joined, the final *u* of the former word is dropped, and the sentence runs—రమ్మను *rammanu*, tell (him) to come. If the words కత్తి *katti*, a knife, and ఎక్కడ *ekkaḍa*, where, come together, the letter య *ya* is inserted, and the sentence runs—కత్తియెక్కడ *katti-yekkaḍa*, where (is) the knife?

38. All Telugu words are divided for this euphonic purpose into two classes. Words in one class are called *kaḷalu*, and those in the other *drutaprakrutulu*.

39. (*a.*) *Kaḷalu.*—Words in the first class insert య *ya*, between the two vowels.

40. This class consists of the following words:

(1.) All nominative cases, with the exception of నేను *nénu*, I, and తాను *tánu*, he; and all the inflexions of nouns.

(2.) The postpositions యొక్క *yokka*, of, గురించి *gurinchi*, concerning, నుంచి *nunchi*, from, and some others.

(3.) The final letters *á*, *é* and *ó*, expressing interrogation, emphasis, and doubt.

(4.) Indeclinable particles.

(5.) All interjections and vocatives.

(6.) The words ఇప్పుడు, అప్పుడు, ఎప్పుడు, *ippuḍu, appuḍu, yeppuḍu,* now, then, and when.

(7.) Every part of the verb, with the exception of the first and third persons singular, and the third neuter plural of the first form of the past tense and of the affirmative aorist; the first person singular of the negative aorist; the infinitive; the present participle ending in చు *tsu;* and the indefinite relative participle ending in డి or డు *ḍi* or *ḍu.*

41. (*b.*) *Drutaprakrutulu.*—Every word not included in the above division is in the class called *drutaprakrutulu.* Words in this class insert the consonant న *na* to prevent hiatus, and it is placed between the opposing vowels for the sake of euphony. The letter న *na* is called *drutamu* or fleeting, from which the above word is derived. Thus: ఇంకనేమి *inkanémi,* what more? The న *na* is here inserted between ఇంక *inka,* more, and ఏమి *émi,* what.

(4.) Sandhi, or Union.

42. Sandhi, union or junction, is the term used in Sanskrit grammar for the elision and combination of vowels which come together. Except in the case of imported Sanskrit words and phrases, the rules of Sandhi as applied to Telugu are few and simple.

43. No words take Sandhi except those ending in *a, i,* or *u.*

(1.) When the final vowel of the first word is *a,* it may either be omitted altogether, and the word joined to the following one by the medial form of the initial vowel of the second word, or య *ya* may be inserted. Thus: మేసిన ఆవు *mésina ávu*, the cow that has grazed, may either become మేసినావు *mésinávu*, or మేసినయావు *mésinayávu*.

44. As a rule, *druta* words ending in *a* do not receive Sandhi, but insert న *na*.

45. (2) Words ending in *i* do not generally take Sandhi. The exceptions are the second person singular of the first form of the past tense ending in తివి *tivi*, and the second person plural ending in తిరి *tiri*.

46. In the pronouns అది *adi*, that, అవి *avi*, those, యిది *idi*, this, యివి *ivi*, these, యేది, యేవి, యేమి *yédi*, *yévi*, *yémi*, which and what, Sandhi is optional.

47. (3.) Words ending in *u*, on the other hand, almost invariably receive Sandhi. There are a few exceptions, which will be readily learned in practice, such as the objective cases of pronouns, నన్ను, నిన్ను, తన్ను, *nannu*, *ninnu*, *tannu*, &c., in which it is optional. Thus: అతడు యిచ్చెను *atadu ichchenu*, he has given, will become అతడిచ్చెను *attadichchenu*.

48. All words ending in the short vowels invariably take Sandhi before the words ఎడు *edu*, full, ఏసి *ési*, at the rate of, అంత *anta*, as much as, ఆకు *áku*, a leaf, and some other common words beginning with a vowel. Thus: మూర *múra*, a cubit, and ఎడు *eḍu*, full, become మూరెడు *múreḍu*, a

cubit full, or the length of a cubit. పది *padi,* ten, and ఏసి *ési,* at the rate of, become పదేసి *padési,* at the rate of ten. తాటి *táṭi,* the inflexion of తాడు *táḍu,* a palmyra tree, and ఆకు *áku,* a leaf, become తాటాకు *táṭáku,* a palmyra leaf or cadjan.

(5.) Permutation or Interchange of Consonants.

49. Many of the consonants in the Telugu language are interchangeable. Even in the commonest intercourse of ordinary conversation these changes constantly occur. A few simple rules are all that is necessary in a work like the present.

50. The letters that are thus interchangeable are క, చ, ట, త, ప, *ka, cha, ṭa, ta, pa,* which are frequently turned into the cognate letters గ, స or జ, డ, ద, వ or బ, *ga, sa* or *ja, ḍa, da, va* or *ba.* It must, however, be borne in mind that the reverse change cannot be admitted, that is to say, గ *ga* cannot be changed into క *ka,* &c.

51. (1.) When words beginning with the above letters are preceded by nouns in the nominative case, and by such parts of the verb as end in డు, దు, or ది, *ḍu, du,* or *di,* as well as by అప్పుడు, యిప్పుడు, యెప్పుడు, *appuḍu, ippuḍu, yeppuḍu,* then, now, when, they are changed into their equivalents గ, స, డ, ద, వ, *ga, sa, ḍa, da, va.* Thus: అది *adi,* that, preceding కాక *káka,* the negative relative participle of అవు *avu,* to become, the కా *ká* is changed into గా *gá,* and produces

the common phrase, అదిగాక *adigáka*, besides that. Again, in the phrase, అన్న *anna*, an elder brother, joined to తమ్ములు *tammulu*, younger brothers, the త *ta* with which the latter word begins is always changed into ద *da*, thus: అన్నదమ్ములు *annadammulu*, brothers. Similarly, తల్లి *talli*, mother, and తండ్రి *tanḍri*, father, together become తల్లిదండ్రులు *tallidanḍrulu*, parents.

52. (2.) When words beginning with the above consonants, namely, క, చ, ట, త, ప, *ka, cha, ṭa, ta, pa,* are preceded by words in the *druta* class, these letters are changed into గ, జ, డ, ద, బ, *ga, ja, ḍa, da, ba.* Thus: in the passive voice, the verb పడు *paḍu*, to fall, in all its moods and tenses, is added to the infinitive of active verbs, and the initial ప *pa* is changed into బ *ba*, the infinitive mood belonging to the *druta* class. The active voice పంపు *pampu*, to send, is changed into the passive by adding పడు *paḍu*, to fall, to the infinitive; but the ప *pa* of the latter is changed into బ *ba*, and the whole word becomes పంపబడు *pampabaḍu*, to be sent.

III. ETYMOLOGY.

(1.) Nouns. (*a.*) Gender.

1. There are three genders in Telugu, namely, masculine, feminine, and neuter. The masculine represents men; the feminine, women; and the neuter, animals and inanimate objects.

(*b.*) Number.

2. There are two numbers—singular and plural. The plural is formed by adding లు *lu* to the nominative singular, or to the inflexion.

(*c.*) Cases.

3. Telugu nouns can scarcely be divided into declensions, and the usual cases of the Latin language are totally inapplicable to them. The best plan will be to arrange them in classes according to their terminations. The only changes in the form of the noun which can properly be called cases are three, namely, the nominative, the inflexion, and the objective. These three cases apply equally to the singular and to the plural. Various forms of the noun showing the relation in which it stands to other words, are indicated by adding to the singular or to the plural inflexion certain postpositions, a list of which will subsequently be given. Some of these suffixes, when added to the inflexion, formerly received the name of cases; but, in that supposition, if, as might justly be done, all of them were so called, the number of such cases would be indefinitely enlarged.

4. As a general rule, the inflexion singular is the same as the nominative, or is formed by changing the nominative into ని *ni* or ను *nu*; and the objective is formed in a similar way; but the variations are so numerous, especially in pure Dravidian words, that no definite rule can be laid down.

5. The nominative plural always ends in లు *lu,* which is either affixed to the nominative singular, or incorporated

with it. Thus: to నరము *naramu,* a nerve, లు *lu* is affixed, making నరములు *naramulu,* nerves; but in చోటు *tsóṭu,* a place, the లు *lu* is incorporated with the singular. Thus: చోట్లు *tsóṭlu,* places. The different classes or groups of nouns must, therefore, be carefully examined.

6. The inflexion plural is invariably formed by changing the *u* into *a,* and the objective by affixing ను *nu* to the inflexion. Thus: నరములు *naramulu,* nerves, is in the inflexion నరముల *naramula,* and in the objective, నరములను, *naramulanu.*

7. Instead therefore of dividing nouns into declensions, with a numerous string of exceptions, we think the most convenient method is to divide them into classes or groups.

(2.) Declension of Nouns.

8. (*a.*) Class 1. Nouns ending in డు *ḍu.*

The first class contains masculine nouns ending in డు *ḍu.* These nouns form the inflexion by changing the termination of the nominative into ని *ni,* and the objective is formed in the same manner.

Singular.

Nominative.	*Inflexion.*	*Objective.*
మనమడు	మనమని	మనమని
manamaḍu	*manamani*	*manamani*
A grandson.		

Plural.

The nominative plural is formed by changing the final డు *ḍu* of the nominative singular into లు *lu;* the inflexion, by changing the *u* of the nominative into *a*; and the objective, by affixing ను *nu* to the inflexion.

Nominative.	*Inflexion.*	*Objective.*
మనమలు	మనమల	మనమలను
manamalu	*manamala*	*manamalanu*
Grandsons.		

9. Some masculine nouns in this group which end in *uḍu*, that is, which have *u* preceding the final డు *ḍu*, have a second mode of forming the inflexion by dropping the డు *ḍu* as well as by changing డు *ḍu* into ని *ni*. Thus: బల్లిదుడు *balliduḍu,* a hero, is in the inflexion either బల్లిదు *ballidu,* or బల్లిదుని *balliduni.* The exceptions are తమ్ముడు *tammuḍu,* a younger brother, and అల్లుడు *alluḍu,* a son-in-law.

(*b.*) Class 2. Nouns in ము *mu.*

10. Neuter nouns ending in ము *mu,* preceded by *a, e,* or *á* are numerous. The inflexion singular is the same as the nominative, though the final *mu* is commonly changed into పు *pu;* and the objective is formed by adding ను *nu,* to the inflexion. The nominative plural is formed by adding లు *lu* to the nominative singular; the inflexion, by changing the final *u* of the nominative into *a;* and the objective, by adding ను *nu* to the inflexion. The usual form of this class of nouns is appended.

SINGULAR.

Nominative.	*Inflexion.*	*Objective.*
గుర్రము	గుర్రము	గుర్రమును
gurramu	*gurramu*	*gurramunu*
A horse.	or గుర్రపు	
	gurrapu	

PLURAL.

గుర్రములు	గుర్రముల	గుర్రములను
gurramulu	*gurramula*	*gurramulanu*
Horses.		

11. Another mode of forming the plural is by lengthening the penultimate syllable and adding *lu*. Thus:

గుర్రాలు	గుర్రాల	గుర్రాలను
gurrálu	*gurrála*	*gurrálanu*
Horses.		

(c.) CLASS 3. NOUNS IN *i*.

12. Nouns ending in *i* remain the same in the inflexion singular as in the nominative, but form the objective by affixing ని *ni* to the nominative. This sign is really the same as ను *nu*, the sign of the objective in other nouns; but the change is made for the sake of euphony, which, to a considerable extent, governs the formation of Dravidian words. For the same reason, in the plural, which is formed in the same manner as other nouns, the final *i* preceding the plural termination లు *lu*, is changed into *u*. Thus:

SINGULAR.

Nominative.	*Inflexion.*	*Objective.*
పులి	పులి	పులిని
puli	*puli*	*pulini*
A tiger.		

PLURAL.

పులులు	పులుల	పులులను
pululu	*pulula*	*pululanu*

13. Nouns which end in టి *ṭi* and డి *ḍi* drop the penultimate *u*, and the sign of the plural, లు *lu*, is joined directly to the preceding consonant. Thus: బండి *banḍi*, a cart, బండ్లు *banḍlu*, carts. Some nouns euphoniously change the final డి *ḍi* of the singular into ళ *ḷa* before the sign of the plural. Thus: కోడి *kóḍi*, a fowl, కోళ్లు *kóḷlu*, fowls.

(*d.*) CLASS 4. NOUNS IN *a*.

14. Nouns ending in *a* remain unaltered in the inflexion, and form the objective singular by affixing ను *nu*, and the plural by adding *lu*. Thus.

SINGULAR.

Nominative.	*Inflexion.*	*Objective.*
అన్న	అన్న	అన్నను
anna	*anna*	*annanu*
An elder brother.		

PLURAL.

అన్నలు	అన్నల	అన్నలను
annalu	*annala*	*annalanu*
Elder brothers.		

(e.) CLASS 5.

15. Several nouns appear to form the inflexion singular and the nominative plural in a very irregular manner; but the principle of forming the inflexion in *i* and the plural in *lu* is throughout very apparent. The various changes made in the letters preceding these terminations, have gradually adapted themselves in the course of ages purely for the sake of euphony. Nouns which appear to us most peculiar are pure Telugu words of the old Dravidian stock on which the whole language is founded, and thus, in their very irregularity, are really more regular than the others. In the following list we give only the nominative and inflexion singular, and the nominative plural. It will be borne in mind that the objective singular is always formed by affixing ని *ni* or ను *nu* to the inflexion singular, and the inflexion plural by changing లు *lu* into ల *la*, and the objective plural by adding ను *nu* to the inflexion.

English.	*Nominative.*	*Inflexion.*	*Plural.*
A river	యేరు *yéru*	యేటి *yéṭi*	యేళ్లు *yéḷlu*
A door	వాకిలి *vákili*	వాకిటి *vákiṭi*	వాకిళ్లు *vákiḷlu*
A field	చేను *chénu*	చేని *chéni*	చేలు *chélu*
A village	వూరు *úru*	వూరి *úri*	వూళ్లు *úḷlu*
An antelope	లేడి *léḍi*	లేటి *léṭi*	లేళ్లు *léḷlu*

16. (*a.*) Some nouns ending in *u* have the inflexion singular regular, while the plural appears to be irregular; but it will be seen at once that the plural is merely a euphonious contraction of what would have been the regular formation. Thus:

English.	*Nominative.*	*Inflexion.*	*Plural.*
A stab	పోటు *póṭu*	పోటు *póṭu*	పోట్లు *póṭlu*
A tree	చెట్టు *cheṭṭu*	చెట్టు *cheṭṭu*	చెట్లు *cheṭlu*

17. (*b.*) Other nouns form the inflexion singular by changing the final syllable of the nominative singular into టి *ṭi*, and in the plural into ళ్లు *ḷlu* or ండ్లు *nḍlu*. Thus:—

English.	*Nominative.*	*Inflexion.*	*Plural.*
A rope	తాడు *táḍu*	తాటి *táṭi*	తాళ్లు *táḷlu*
A yard	పెరడు *peraḍu*	పెరటి *peraṭi*	పెరళ్లు *peraḷlu*
A nest	గూడు *gúḍu*	గూటి *gúṭi*	గూళ్లు *gúḷlu*

18. (*c.*) Others change the last syllable of the nominative singular into ంటి *nti* for the inflexion, and into ంళ్లు *nḷlu* or ండ్లు *nḍlu* in the plural. Thus:

English.	*Nominative.*	*Inflexion.*	*Plural.*
A house	యిల్లు *illu*	యింటి *inṭi*	యిండ్లు or యిళ్లు *inḍlu* or *iḷlu*
A bow	విల్లు *villu*	వింటి *vinṭi*	విండ్లు *vinḍlu*

English.	*Nominative.*	*Inflexion.*	*Plural.*
A thorn	ముల్లు *mullu*	ముంటి *munṭi*	ముండ్లు *munḍlu*
A tooth	పల్లు *pallu*	పంటి *panṭi*	పండ్లు *panḍlu*
The eye	కన్ను *kannu*	కంటి *kanṭi*	కండ్లు *kanḍlu*

19. (*d.*) The nominative singular of some nouns remains unchanged in the inflexion, or the last syllable is changed into టి *ṭi;* and the plural is formed either by adding లు *lu* to the nominative singular, or by changing the last syllable into ళ్లు *ḷlu.* Thus:

English.	*Nominative.*	*Inflexion.*	*Plural.*
A mortar	రోలు *rólu*	రోలు or రోటి *rólu* or *róṭi*	రోలులు or రోళ్లు *rólulu* or *róḷlu*

20. (*e.*) Some pure Telugu words change the last syllable of the nominative singular into తి *ti* to form the inflexion, and into తులు *tulu* to form the plural, those words in which the penultimate is short having it lengthened in the inflexion and in the plural. Thus:

English.	*Nominative.*	*Inflexion.*	*Plural.*
A well	నుయ్యి *nuyy*	నూతి *núti*	నూతులు *nútulu*
A pit	గొయ్యి *goyy*	గోతి *góti*	గోతులు *gótulu*
The hand	చెయ్యి *cheyy*	చేతి *chéti*	చేతులు *chétulu*

21. (*f.*) Some nouns ending in *u* change the *u* into *i* in the inflexion, and into *lu* or *ḷlu* in the plural. Thus:

English.	*Nominative.*	*Inflexion*	*Plural.*
The leg	కాలు *kálu*	కాలి *káli*	కాళ్లు *káḷlu*
A field	చేను *chénu*	చేని *chéni*	చేలు *chélu*
A finger	వేలు *vélu*	వేలి *véli*	వేళ్లు *véḷlu*
A tree	మాను *mánu*	మాని *máni*	మానులు *mánulu*

22. (*g.*) Nouns ending in ఱు *rru* form the inflexion in ర్తి *rti*, and the plural in లు *lu* or ర్లు *rlu*. Thus:

English.	*Nominative.*	*Inflexion.*	*Plural.*
A ploughshare	కఱు *karru*	కర్తి *karti*	కఱులు *karrulu*
A certain extent of land	గొఱు *gorru*	గొర్తి *gorti*	గొర్లు *gorlu*

23. Many of these words have a locative or instrumental case peculiar to themselves, which is formed by changing the final *i* of the inflexion into *a*. This case is employed either instead of, or in addition to, the use of the postpositions లో *ló* or తో *tó* when affixed to the inflexion. Thus:

English.	*Nom. Sing.*	*Inflexion.*	*Locative.*
A nest	గూడు *gúḍu*	గూటి *gúṭi*	గూట *gúṭa*
A door	వాకిలి *vákili*	వాకిటి *vákiṭi*	వాకిట *vákiṭa*

English.	*Nominative.*	*Inflexion.*	*Locative.*
A house	యిల్లు *illu*	యింటి *inṭi*	యింట *inṭa*
A mortar	రోలు *rólu*	రోటి *róti*	రోట *róta*
The hand	చెయ్యి *cheyy*	చేతి *chéti*	చేత *chéta*

24. Several of these words, all being of the pure Dravidian stock, have the same plurals, and it is expedient that the student should have this fact pointed out to him, although he would soon discover it in practice. Thus:

Nom. Singular.	*Nom. Plural.*
వేరు *véru*, a root వేలు *vélu*, a finger	వేళ్లు
పండు *panḍu*, a fruit పల్లు *pallu*, a tooth	పండ్లు
నాడు *náḍu*, a day నాడు *náḍu*, a country నాడి *náḍi*, a nerve	నాళ్లు

THE VOCATIVE.

25. In addressing others and calling the attention of any one to anything, the sign *ó* or *óyi* is used, and the final syllable of the nominative, singular or plural, is lengthened, and, in the plural, the syllable రా *rá* is added. Thus:

ఓ తమ్ముడా, *ó tammuḍá*, O brother.

ఓ తండ్రీ, *ó tanḍrí*, O father.

ఓ తండ్రులారా, *ó tanḍrulárá*, O fathers.

(3.) Postpositions.

26. According to the genius of the Telugu language, nouns can be utilized to almost any extent by the employment of suffixes or postpositions, which, as a general rule, are affixed to the inflexion. The principal postpositions are subjoined; but the limited space in a simplified grammar like the present does not permit of an exhaustive list being given.

Postposition.	*Transliteration.*	*English.*
కి or కు	*ki* or *ku,*	To or for
కోసరము	*kósaramu,*	for
కొరకు	*koraku,*	for
చేత	*chéta,*	by
తో	*tó*	with
లో	*ló*	in or at
లోపల	*lópala*	within
లోకి	*lóki*	into
న	*na*	in or on
పయిన	*paina*	above
మీద	*mída*	upon
కింద	*kinda*	below
గుండా	*gundá*	through
దగ్గర	*daggira*	near
ముందర	*mundara*	before
వెనక	*venaka*	behind

27. Observations. కి or కు *ki* or *ku*, for. The former is affixed to inflexions ending in *i*, and the latter to those ending in any other vowel. Thus: తండ్రి *tanḍri*, a father; తండ్రికి *tanḍriki*, to a father. అన్న *anna*, an elder brother; అన్నకు *annaku*, to an elder brother.

28. In the case of nouns ending in ము *mu*, న *na* is inserted, for the sake of euphony, between the ము *mu* and కు *ku*. Thus: గుర్రము *gurramu*, a horse, గుర్రమునకు *gurramunaku*, to a horse; or else the penultimate is lengthened, ని *ni* inserted and కి *ki* affixed. Thus: గుర్రానికి, *gurrániki*, to a horse.

29. Some of these postpositions are doubled, or joined together, in natural combination, as is the case with the English prepositions, as, for example, into, with which లోకి *lóki*, into, compounded of లో *ló*, in, and కి *ki*, to, exactly corresponds. Thus: లో *ló* and నుంచి *nunchi*, లోనుంచి *lónunchi*, from within.

30. The postposition యొక్క *yokka*, of, is sometimes inserted between the inflexion and the noun which governs it. Thus: తల్లిప్రేమ *talli préma*, or తల్లియొక్కప్రేమ *talliyokka préma*, a mother's love. The latter is seldom used.

31. Some postpositions are affixed to the objective case instead of to the inflexion. Thus: గురించి *gurinchi*, concerning or about. తండ్రినిగురించి *tanḍrini gurinchi*, about the father.

(4.) *PRONOUNS.*

32. The pronouns in Telugu are (i) the Personal, (ii) the Demonstrative, (iii) the Reflective, (iv) the Interrogative, (v) and the Collective. There is no separate relative pronoun, the nature of the language requiring the English relative pronoun to be expressed by one of the participial forms of the verb.

(i.) Personal Pronouns.

33. The personal pronouns are declined exactly like nouns. They have two numbers, and three cases, both in the singular and in the plural. The pronouns, like the nouns, can be utilized to any extent by the use of the postpositions affixed to the inflexion, or, in some instances, to the objective.

34. Very great care should be exercised in the use of the singular or the plural pronouns. The plural is always used in addressing an equal or a superior, the singular being either very disrespectful or very loving and familiar. The nice and careful distinction in the number can be obtained only by close intercourse with the people themselves; and, in conversation, it requires much tact and courteous discrimination to prevent unintentional offence. The honorific plural should always be used in writing to or speaking of those in authority, గారు *gáru*, a polite honorific affix, being always added to the name of the person spoken of or addressed.

1. *The First Personal Pronoun.*

35. The first personal pronoun is నేను *nénu,* I. The inflexion singular is నా *ná,* and the objective నన్ను *nannu.* The nominative plural is మేము *mému,* the inflexion మా *má,* and the objective మమ్ము.

	Singular.			*Plural.*		
Nominative	నేను	*nénu*	I	మేము	*mému*	we
Inflexion	నా	*ná*	me	మా	*má*	us
Objcctive	నన్ను	*nannu*	me	మమ్ము	*mammu*	us

36. With the addition of the postpositions to the inflexion the same variety of combinations can be made as in the case of nouns. Thus: నాతో *nátó,* with me; మాచేత *máchéta,* by us. Or by addition to the objective, as, నన్నుగురించి *nannugurinchi,* concerning me.

37. The English possessive 'my,' 'thy,' 'his,' &c., is formed by placing the inflexion of the pronoun before the noun which it is intended to qualify; as, నా గుఱ్ఱము *ná gurramu,* my horse.

38. There is a second plural, or dual, of the first personal pronoun, which includes both the speaker and the person or persons addressed. Thus:

	Plural.		
Nominative	మనము	*manamu*	we
Inflexion	మన	*mana*	us
Objective	మనముల	*manamula*	us

2. *Second Personal Pronoun.*

39. The second personal pronoun is నీవు *nívu,* thou. The cases are formed in a similar way to those of the first personal pronoun, *í* being substituted for *á*. Thus:

	Singular.			Plural.		
Nominative	నీవు	*nívu*	thou	మీరు	*míru*	ye
Inflexion	నీ	*ní*	thee	మీ	*mí*	you
Objective	నిన్ను	*ninnu*	thee	మిమ్ము	*mimmu*	you

40. It may be noticed here that in adding the postposition కు *ku* to the inflexion, it is not changed into కి *ki* according to the usual custom, but is affixed without alteration. Thus: నీకు *níku,* to thee; మీకు *míku,* to you.

3. *Third Personal Pronoun.*

41. The third personal pronoun is represented by several words, which differ from each other according to the nearness or remoteness of the person referred to with reference to the person speaking; or as to the position in society of the person mentioned with reference to the speaker.

42. The particles *í* and *á* prefixed to neuter nouns indicate the English pronouns 'this' and 'that.' Thus: ఈ గుర్రము *í gurramu,* this horse; ఆ గుర్రము *á gurramu,* that horse.

43. As a general rule, this distinction runs through all the pronouns of the third person, *i* or *í* and *a* or *á* being

characteristic of the pronouns according to the nearness or remoteness of the thing or person indicated. Thus: వీడు *víḍu,* ఇతడు *itaḍu,* ఈయన *íyana* are 'this person,' nearness being implied: వాడు *váḍu,* అతడు *ataḍu,* ఆయన *áyana,* 'that person,' remoteness being indicated.

44. The gender in the third Telugu pronoun is very peculiar. The feminine and neuter singular are alike, while the feminine and masculine plural are the same. Thus: ఇది *idi,* this woman or this thing, అది *adi,* that woman or that thing, వీరు *víru,* these men or these women, వారు *váru,* those men or those women. This peculiarity should be clearly understood and firmly grasped, as it influences the formation of the adjectives and verbs, and affects the construction of sentences.

(ii.) Demonstrative Pronouns.

(*a.*) వీడు *víḍu,* this man, he.

45. The inflexion and objective singular are formed by changing the final డు *ḍu* of the nominative into ని *ni*; and the nominative plural is formed by changing the డు *ḍu* of the nominative singular into రు *ru,* the inflexion by changing the రు *ru* of the nominative into రి *ri,* and the objective by adding ని *ni* to the inflexion. Thus:

	Masculine Sing.			*Mas. & Fem. Plural.*		
Nominative	వీడు	*víḍu*	he	వీరు	*víru*	they
Inflexion	వీని	*víni*	him	వీరి	*víri*	them
Objective	వీని	*víni*	him	వీరిని	*vírini*	them

(*b.*) వాడు *váḍu*, that man, he.

Nominative	వాడు	*váḍu*	he	వారు	*váru*	they
Inflexion	వాని	*váni*	him	వారి	*vári*	them
Objective	వాని	*váni*	him	వారిని	*várini*	them

46. There is a second form of the plural, which is very common, especially in conversation, but not so elegant as the above. Thus:

Nominative	వీండ్లు	*vínḍlu*	వాండ్లు	*vánḍlu*
Inflexion	వీండ్ల	*vínḍla*	వాండ్ల	*vánḍla*
Objective	వీండ్లను	*vínḍlanu*	వాండ్లను	*vánḍlanu*

47. (*c.*) ఇది *idi*, and అది *adi*, she and it.

	Fem. & Neut. Sing.		*Neut. Plural.*		
Nominative	ఇది	*idi*	ఇవి	*ivi*	These things.
Inflexion	దీని	*díni*	వీటి	*víṭi*	
Objective	దీని	*díni*	వీటిని	*víṭini*	
Nominative	అది	*adi*	అవి	*avi*	Those things.
Inflexion	దాని	*dáni*	వాటి	*váṭi*	
Objective	దాని	*dáni*	వాటిని	*váṭini*	

48. The above pronouns are used in speaking of or addressing inferiors. The pronouns అతడు *ataḍu* and ఆయన *áyana*, ఇతడు *itaḍu* and ఈయన *íyana*, he, and ఈమె and ఈబిడ *íme* and *íbiḍa*, ఆమె and ఆబిడ *áme* and *ábiḍa*, she, are used when the person spoken of or addressed is superior to the person speaking. They represent gradations of respect, ఇతడు *itaḍu* and అతడు *ataḍu* being less respectful than ఈయన *íyana* and ఆయన *áyana*, which should always be used in speaking of those high in rank. As in the other pronouns, *i* and *a* represent nearness or remoteness. They are declined as follows, there being no plural.

Nominative	ఇతడు	అతడు	*itaḍu*,	*ataḍu*	he.
Inflexion	ఇతని	అతని	*itani*,	*atani*	him.
Objective	ఇతని	అతని	*itani*,	*atani*	him.
Nominative	ఈయన	ఆయన	*íyana*,	*áyana*	he.
Inflexion	ఈయన	ఆయన	*íyana*,	*áyana*	him.
Objective	ఈయనను	ఆయనను	*íyananu*,	*áyananu*	him.
Nominative	ఈమె	*íme*,	ఈబిడ	*íbiḍa*	she.
Inflexion	ఈమె	*íme*,	ఈబిడ	*íbiḍa*	her.
Objective	ఈమెను	*ímenu*,	ఈబిడను	*íbiḍanu*	her.

(iii.) REFLECTIVE PRONOUNS.

49. There is likewise a reflective pronoun of the third person, which always refers to some noun or pronoun that precedes it, irrespective of gender. తాను *tánu*, he, she, or it, is thus declined:

	Singular.			Plural.		
Nom.	తాను	*tánu*	he, she, it	తాము	*támu,*	they
Inf.	తన	*tana*	him, her, it	తమ	*tama,*	them
Obj.	తన్ను	*tannu*	him, her, it	తమ్మును	*tammunu,*	them.

50. There is another form of the nominative plural, namely, తమరు *tamaru.* Both plurals also signify 'you,' and are used in addressing a superior.

(iv.) Interrogative Pronouns.

51. As ఈ *í* and ఆ *á* are used before neuter nouns to represent 'this' and 'that,' so the letter ఏ *é* is used to represent 'which.' Thus: ఏ పుస్తకము *é pustakamu,* which book?

52. The ordinary interrogative pronouns are, masculine, ఎవడు *evaḍu,* who; feminine, ఎవతె *evate,* who; and feminine and neuter, ఏది *édi,* which. They are declined as follows:

	Mas. Sing.		Mas. & Fem. Plu.		
Nominative	ఎవడు	*evaḍu*	ఎవరు	*evaru*	who
Inflexion	ఎవని	*evani*	ఎవరి	*evari*	whom
Objective	ఎవని	*evani*	ఎవరిని	*evarini*	whom.

Feminine ఎవతె *evate,* who.

Nominative	ఎవతె	*evate*	who
Inflexion	ఎవతె	*evate*	whom
Objective	ఎవతెను	*evatenu*	whom.

ఏది *édi*, which.

	Fem. & Neut. Sing.		*Neut. Plural.*	
Nominative	ఏది	*édi*	ఏవి	*évi*
Inflexion	దేని	*déni*	వేటి	*véṭi*
Objective	దేని	*déni*	వేటిని	*véṭini*

53. Numerous compound nouns are formed by the combination of the above pronouns with adjectives, and they are then declined like the pronouns themselves. Thus: ముసలివాడు *musaliváḍu*, an old man, వాడు *váḍu*, he, being added to the adjective ముసలి *musali*, old. చిన్నవాడు *chinna-vádu*, a little boy, చిన్నది *chinnadi*, a little girl. నాది, *ná adi*, contracted into *nádi*, mine, lit. 'it of me.'

(v.) Collective Pronouns.

54. There are several pronouns of number, which are declined like the ordinary personal pronouns, and, though they really partake very much of the nature of adjectives of quantity, they fall more naturally into their place among the pronouns. They are connected with the adverbs ఇందు, అందు, ఎందు, *indu, andu, endu*, in this place, in that place, where or in what place; and have the same signs of nearness, remoteness, and interrogation as the pronouns.

They are ఇందరు, అందరు, ఎందరు, and కొందరు, *indaru*, so many, *andaru*, all, *endaru*, how many, and *kondaru*, some. They are all declined alike. Thus:

	Masc. & Fem.		*Neuter.*	
Nominative	ఇందరు	*indaru*	ఇన్ని	*inni*
Inflexion	ఇందరి	*indari*	ఇన్నిటి	*inniṭi*
Objective	ఇందరిని	*indarini*	ఇన్నిటిని	*inniṭini*

(5.) *ADJECTIVES.*

55. Pure Telugu adjectives, which are generally short and simple words ending in *a, i,* or *u,* are prefixed unchanged to the nouns they qualify, without reference to number or gender. Thus: చెడ్డ మనిషి *cheḍḍa manishi,* a bad man; మంచి పండు *manchi panḍu,* a good fruit; మంచి నీళ్లు *manchi níḷlu,* good water.

56. ని *ni* is added, at pleasure, to most adjectives ending in *a* denoting objects of sense. Thus: పచ్చని పువ్వు *patstsani puvvu,* a yellow flower; చల్లని గాలి *tsallani gáli,* a cold wind. చక్క *tsakka,* handsome, always has ని *ni* affixed to it. Thus: చక్కని మనిషి *tsakkani manishi,* a handsome man.

57. అయిన *aina,* అయినటువంటి, *ainaṭuvanṭi,* or అగు *agu* are sometimes added to adjectives ending in *u,* before the noun they qualify; or the final ము *mu* is changed into పు. Thus: అందము *andamu,* beautiful, is changed before a noun into అందమగు, అందమైన, అందమైనటువంటి, or అందపు, *andamagu, andamaina, andamainaṭuvanṭi,* or *andapu*— అందమైన మొగము *andamaina mogamu,* a handsome face.

58. Adjectives are sometimes placed after the nouns they qualify, when the verb 'to be' is understood; and, then, the masculine or the feminine and neuter demonstrative pronoun is added. Thus: ఆ బ్రాహ్మణుడు గుడ్డివాడు *á Bráhmaṇuḍu guḍḍiváḍu,* that Brahman (is) blind; ఆ గుర్రము మంచిది *á gurramu manchidi,* that (is) a good horse.

59. Though generally placed before the nouns they qualify, adjectives are sometimes placed after them. Thus: భూమి గుండ్రము *bhúmi gunḍramu,* the earth (is) round.

60. Adjectives are frequently formed from nouns by affixing to them the particle గల *gala,* being the irregular past participle of the verb కలుగు *kalugu,* to be, the initial క *k* being changed into గ *g.* Thus: జాగ్రత *jágrata,* care, జాగ్రతగల *jágratagala,* careful.

(*a.*) DEGREES OF COMPARISON.

61. There are really no degrees of comparison in Telugu, the genius of the language not admitting of them. They are expressed by a periphrasis.

(i.) *The Comparative Degree.*

62. The English comparative is expressed by the term కన్న *kanna* or కంటే *kanṭé,* than, being placed before the adjective. Thus: ఇంతకంటే మంచిది లేదు *intakanṭé manchidi lédu,* there is nothing better than this, literally, nothing is good than this.

(ii.) *The Superlative Degree.*

63. The superlative degree is expressed by అందరికంటే *andari kanṭé*, than all, in the masculine and feminine, and అన్నిటికంటే *annitikanṭé* in the neuter. Thus: అతడు అందరికంటే మంచివాడు *atadu andarikanṭé manchiváḍu*, he is the best man; ఇది అన్నిటికంటే గొప్పది *idi anniṭi kanṭé goppadi*, this is the largest, literally, this is large than all the things.

(6.) *NUMERALS.*

64. The Telugu numerals are divided into cardinals and ordinals.

(*a.*) *Cardinal Numbers.*

65. The following are the cardinal numbers arranged both in figures and letters with their English equivalents.

ENGLISH.		TELUGU.	
Figures.	*Letters.*	*Figures.*	*Letters.*
1	One	౧	ఒకటి *okaṭi*
2	Two	౨	రెండు *renḍu*
3	Three	౩	మూడు *múḍu*
4	Four	౪	నాలుగు *nálugu*
5	Five	౫	అయిదు *aidu*

English.		Telugu.	
Figures.	*Letters.*	*Figures.*	*Letters.*
6	Six	౬	ఆరు *áru*
7	Seven	౭	ఏడు *yéḍu*
8	Eight	౮	ఎనిమిది *yenimidi*
9	Nine	౯	తొమ్మిది *tommidi*
10	Ten	౧౦	పది *padi*
11	Eleven	౧౧	పదకొండు *padakonḍu*
12	Twelve	౧౨	పన్నెండు *pannenḍu*
13	Thirteen	౧౩	పదమూడు *padamúḍu*
14	Fourteen	౧౪	పధ్నాలుగు *padhnálugu*
15	Fifteen	౧౫	పదిహేను *padihénu*
16	Sixteen	౧౬	పదహారు *padaháru*
17	Seventeen	౧౭	పదిహేడు *padihéḍu*

English		Telugu	
Figures.	*Letters.*	*Figures.*	*Letters.*
18	Eighteen	౧౮	పద్దెనిమిది *paddenimidi*
19	Nineteen	౧౯	పంతొమ్మిది *pantommidi*
20	Twenty	౨౦	ఇరువై *iruvai*
21	Twenty-one	౨౧	ఇరువైవొకటి *iruvai vokaṭi, &c.*
30	Thirty	౩౦	ముప్పై *muppai*
40	Forty	౪౦	నలుభై *nalubhai*
50	Fifty	౫౦	ఏభై *ébhai*
60	Sixty	౬౦	అరువై *aruvai*
70	Seventy	౭౦	డెబ్భై *ḍebbhai*
80	Eighty	౮౦	ఎనభై *enabhai*
90	Ninety	౯౦	తొంభై *tombhai*
100	Hundred	౧౦౦	నూరు *núru*

English.		Telugu.	
Figures.	*Letters.*	*Figures.*	*Letters.*
200	Two hundred	౨౦౦	ఇన్నూరు *innúru*
300	Three hundred	౩౦౦	మున్నూరు *munnúru*
400	Four hundred	౪౦౦	నన్నూరు *nannúru*
500	Five hundred	౫౦౦	ఏనూరు *énúru*
600	Six hundred	౬౦౦	ఆర్నూరు *árnúru*
700	Seven hundred	౭౦౦	ఏడ్నూరు *éḍnúru*
800	Eight hundred	౮౦౦	ఎనమన్నూరు *enamannúru*
900	Nine hundred	౯౦౦	తొమ్మన్నూరు *tommannúru*
1000	Thousand	౧౦౦౦	వెయ్యి *veyy*
100,000	A lakh	౧,౦౦,౦౦౦	లక్ష *laksha*
10,000,000	A crore	౧,౦౦,౦౦,౦౦౦	కోటి *kóṭi.*

66. When the numeral ఒక *oka,* a or one, is used as an adjective, it is placed before the noun it qualifies unchanged,

irrespective of gender, thus: ఒకమనిషి *oka manishi*, a man; but, when it is used as a substantive, it has a separate form for each gender, and is declined like a noun. Thus:

	Masc.	*Fem.*	*Neut.*
Nom.	ఒకఁడు *okaḍu*	ఒకతె *okate*	ఒకటి *okaṭi*
Infl.	ఒకని *okani*	ఒకతె *okate*	ఒకటి *okaṭi*
Obj.	ఒకని *okani*	ఒకతెను *okatenu*	ఒకటిని *okaṭini*

67. The neuter numerals రెండు *renḍu*, two, మూఁడు *múḍu*, three, నాలుగు *nálugu*, four, become ఇద్దరు *iddaru*, ముగ్గురు *mugguru*, and నలుగురు *naluguru* in the masculine and feminine; and the remaining numbers are rendered masculine or feminine by affixing either గురు *guru* or మంది *mandi* to the neuter. Thus: అయిదుగురు *aiduguru*, five persons, ఆరుమంది మనుష్యులు *árumandi manushyulu*, six men.

68. The masculine and feminine plurals thus formed in రు *ru* are declinable. As:

Nominative	ఇద్దరు *iddaru*	ముగ్గురు *mugguru*
Inflexion	ఇద్దరి *iddari*	ముగ్గురి *mugguri*
Objective	ఇద్దరిని *iddarini*	ముగ్గురిని *muggurini*

69. In counting 'one' after a higher figure, the noun is put in the singular. Thus: ఇరువైవకగుర్రము *iruvai vaka gurramu*, twenty-one horses.

70. రెండు, మూడు, నూరు *reṇḍu, múḍu, núru*, two, three, and a hundred, take an inflexion in టి *ṭi*, రెంటి *renṭi*, మూటి *múṭi*, నూటి *núṭi*, to which some postpositions can be affixed. Thus: నూటికి వకరూపాయి చొప్పున వడ్డి, *núṭiki vaka rúpáy tsoppuna vaḍḍi*, interest at one per cent.

71. In composition వెయ్యి *veyy*, a thousand, has న్ని *nni* added to it, and నూరు *núru*, a hundred, is put into the locative inflexion. Thus: వెయ్యిన్ని నూట నలుభై *veyynni-núṭa-nalubhai*, a thousand, one hundred and forty.

(*b*.) ORDINAL NUMERALS.

72. The ordinal numerals are formed by changing the final vowel of the neuter cardinal numeral into *ó*. అవ *ava* is sometimes used in books and in polished conversation. Thus: రెండో or రెండవ *renḍó* or *renḍava*, second; మూడో *múḍó*; నాలుగో *nálugó*; అయిదో *aidó*; &c.

73. The only exception is the first cardinal, ఒకటి *okaṭi*, which has an entirely different word substituted for it, namely, మొదటి *modaṭi*, unless another number precedes it, when ఒకటో *okaṭó* is used. Thus: ఇరువైవొకటో *iruvai vokaṭó*, the twenty-first. ఈ వరసలో మొదటిమనిషి *í varasaḷó modaṭi manishi*, the first man in this row.

(7.) *VERBS.*

74. The structure of the Telugu verb is strictly agglutinative. "The particles," says Bishop Caldwell in writing of the verb in all the Dravidian languages, "which express

the ideas of mood, tense, causation, and negation, together with the pronominal fragments by which person, number, and gender are denoted, are annexed to the root in so regular a series and by so quiet a process that generally no change whatever, or at most only a slightly euphonic change, is effected in the root." ("Grammar of the Dravidian Languages." 2nd Ed. p. 339).

75. As the Telugu noun has really no clear distinction of declension, so the Telugu verb can scarcely be said to have properly more than one conjugation. Telugu roots are generally short and simple. They always end in *u*. In the original Dravidian stock from which they are derived, they may very probably have ended in consonants; but, as already remarked, the genius of the language demands that every word should end in a vowel, and the addition of *u* imparts breadth and sweetness to the sound, while it scarcely increases the length of the root.

76. The verbs are transitive and intransitive, as, కొట్టు *koṭṭu*, to beat; వెళ్లు *veḷlu*, to go.

77. They have really only three moods—the indicative, infinitive, and imperative; and only three tenses—the present, the perfect, and the aorist. Other moods and tenses as known in English are formed by the careful use of participles, and of auxiliary verbs.

78. There are two numbers—the singular and the plural, and three persons.

79. The root is used as the imperative mood, and all the verbal formations circle round it. The most useful and im-

portant are the participles. The present participle is formed by affixing తు or చు *tu* or *tsu* to the root, and the past participle, by changing the vowel *u* into *i*. Thus: చెప్పు *cheppu*, to speak, చెప్పుచు or చెప్పుతు *chepputsu* or *chepputu*, speaking, చెప్పి *cheppi*, having spoken.

80. The tenses are formed by affixing to the participles, with euphonic agglutination, the fragmentary, but essential, letters of the personal pronouns, namely, ను *nu* for the first person singular, being a fragment of నేను *nénu*, I; వు *vu* for the second person, a fragment of నీవు *nívu*, thou; డు *ḍu*, for the third person masculine, from వాడు *váḍu*, he; ది *di* for the third person neuter, a fragment of ఇది *idi*, this; ము *mu*, for the first person plural, from మేము *mému*, we; రు *ru*, for the second and third persons plural, from మీరు and వారు, *míru* and *váru*, you and they; and వి *vi*, for the third person plural, from ఇవి *ivi*, these. Thus: చెప్పుతు *chepputu*, speaking, is the present participle, and the pronominal fragments being affixed to it, the present tense is thus formed, చెప్పుతాను *chepputánu*, I speak or will speak; చెప్పుతావు *chepputávu*, thou speakest, or will speak; చెప్పుతాడు *chepputáḍu*, he speaks or will speak; చెప్పుతున్నది *chepputunnadi*, it speaks or will speak, &c. The following little form may at first help the memory to retain these pronominal terminations:

Nu - vu - ḍu - di
Mu - ru - ru - vi.

81. The future is generally expressed by using the present tense, and sometimes by employing the aorist. There is a separate form for the future; but, as it is hardly ever used in conversation or in writing simple prose, it is not given here.

82. The regular formation of an ordinary verb, is now given, and the common word 'to speak,' or, 'to say' is selected, which will lend itself as readily as any other, to the reception of the usual terminations.

ACTIVE VOICE.

(i.) చెప్పు *cheppu*, to say.

(*a.*) *AFFIRMATIVE FORM.*

INDICATIVE MOOD. PRESENT TENSE.

83. The Present Indicative is formed by affixing the pronominal fragments to the present participle. Thus:

SINGULAR.

1.	చెప్పుతున్నాను	*chepputu-nnánu,*	I say.
	or చెప్పుతాను	*chepput(u)-ánu*	
2.	చెప్పుతున్నావు	*chepputu-nnávu,*	thou sayest.
	or చెప్పుతావు	*chepput(u)-ávu*	
3.	M. చెప్పుతున్నాడు	*chepputu-nnáḍu,*	he says.
	or చెప్పుతాడు	*chepput(u)-áḍu*	
	F. & N. చెప్పుతున్నది	*cheputu-nnadi,*	she or it says.
	or చెప్పుతుంది	*chepputu-ndi*	

Plural.

1.	చెప్పుతున్నాము	*chepputu-nnámu,*	we say.
	or చెప్పుతాము	*chepput(u)-ámu*	
2.	చెప్పుతున్నారు	*chepputu-nnáru,*	ye say.
	or చెప్పుతారు	*chepput(u)-áru*	
3.	M. & F. చెప్పుతున్నారు	*chepputu-nnáru,*	they say.
	or చెప్పుతారు	*chepput(u)-áru*	
	N. చెప్పుతున్నవి	*chepputu-nnavi,*	they say.

Past Tense.

84. The past tense is formed by affixing the pronominal suffixes to the past participle in a slightly altered form; but it will be observed that the characteristic of each personal pronoun is strictly retained.

Singular.

1.	చెప్పినాను	*cheppi-nánu,*	I have said.
	or చెప్పితిని	*cheppi-tini*	
2.	చెప్పినావు	*cheppi-návu,*	thou hast said.
	or చెప్పితివి	*cheppi-tivi*	
3.	M. చెప్పినాడు	*cheppi-náḍu,*	he has said.
	or చెప్పెను	*chepp(i)-enu*	
	F. & N. చెప్పినది	*cheppi-nadi,*	she or it has said.
	or చెప్పెను	*chepp(i)-enu*	

PLURAL.

1.	చెప్పినాము	*cheppi-námu,*	we have said.
	or చెప్పితిమి	*cheppi-timi*	
2.	చెప్పినారు	*cheppi-náru,*	ye have said.
	or చెప్పితిరి	*cheppi-tiri*	
3.	M. & F. చెప్పినారు	*cheppi-náru,*	they have said.
	or చెప్పిరి	*cheppi-ri*	
	N. చెప్పినవి	*cheppi-navi,*	they have said.
	or చెప్పెను	*chepp(i)-enu*	

AORIST.

85. The aorist is formed by adding the following forms of the pronominal suffixes to the root.

	SINGULAR.	PLURAL.
1.	దును *dunu*	దుము *dumu*
2.	దువు *duvu*	దురు *duru*
3.	M. F. & N. ను *nu*	M. & F. దురు *duru* N. ను *nu*

SINGULAR.

1.	చెప్పుదును	*cheppu-dunu,*	I said.
2.	చెప్పుదువు	*cheppu-duvu,*	thou saidest.
3.	M. F. & N. చెప్పును	*cheppu-nu,*	he said.

PLURAL.

1.	చెప్పితిమి	*cheppu-dumu,*	we said.
2.	చెప్పితిరి	*cheppu-duru,*	ye said.
3.	M. & F. చెప్పిరి	*cheppu-duru,*	they said.
	N. చెప్పెను	*cheppu-nu,*	they said.

INFINITIVE MOOD.

86. The infinitive mood is formed by changing the final *u* of the root into *a*. Thus: చెప్పు *cheppu* is, in the infinitive, changed into చెప్ప *cheppa,* to say.

IMPERATIVE MOOD.

87. The second person singular of the imperative is the same as the root; and the first person plural is formed by adding దాము *dámu* to the root, and the third person plural by changing the final *u* of the root into అండి *anḍi.* ము *mu* is sometimes added to the root to express the second person singular. There is no separate form for the first and third persons singular; but ఇయ్యి *iyy,* the imperative of ఇచ్చు *itstsu,* to give, is added to the infinitive of the verb to express permission. Thus:

SINGULAR.

1.	నన్ను చెప్పనియ్యి	*nannu cheppaniyy,*	let me say; *lit.* give me to say.
2.	చెప్పు or చెప్పుము	*cheppu* or *cheppumu,*	say thou.
3.	వాని చెప్పనియ్యి	*váni cheppaniyy,*	let him say.

Plural.

చెప్పుదాము	*cheppudámu,*	let us say.
2. చెప్పండి	*cheppanḍi,*	say ye.

Relative Participles.

88. As already stated, when describing the pronouns, there are no relative pronouns in Telugu; but the force of these English pronouns is expressed by the relative participles, which are singularly flexible and pliant.

89. The present relative participle is formed by adding న్న *nna* to the present participle.

90. The past relative participle is formed by adding న *na* to the past participle.

91. The indefinite relative participle is formed by changing the final *u* of the root into *é*.

Present participle.	*Present relative participle.*
చెప్పుతు *chepputu*	చెప్పుతున్న *chepputu-nna,* that says.
Past participle.	*Past relative participle.*
చెప్పి *cheppi*	చెప్పిన *cheppi-na,* that has said.
The root	*Indefinite relative participle.*
చెప్పు *cheppu*	చెప్పే *cheppé,* that says, said, or will say.

VERBAL NOUNS.

92. The verbal nouns are formed in three ways—by adding డము *ḍamu* to the infinitive; ట *ṭa* to the root; or ది *di* to the indefinite relative participle. Thus:

చెప్పడము	*cheppa-ḍamu*	The saying.
చెప్పుట	*cheppu-ṭa*	
చెప్పేది	*cheppé-di*	

They are all used as nouns, and are declined like the nouns or pronouns they resemble. Thus: చెప్పడము is declined like nouns ending in ము *mu*, the inflexion being చెప్పడము *cheppaḍamu*, and the objective చెప్పడమును. చెప్పేది *cheppédi*, the thing that is said, is declined like the third neuter personal pronoun, the inflexion being చెప్పేదాని *cheppédáni*, and the objective also చెప్పేదాని. They receive the usual postpositions, as చెప్పడమునకు *cheppaḍamunaku*, చెప్పేదానికి *cheppédaniki*.

(b.) *NEGATIVE FORM.*

93. Negation, as applied to verbs, is not expressed in Telugu by particles or adverbs, but by a distinct form of the verb itself, the pronominal suffixes slightly differing from those in the affirmative form, though easily recognisable as distinctive of each person; or by adding to the infinitive certain parts of the irregular verb, ఉండు *unḍu*, to be. It will be observed that *a* is the key-letter of the negative form of the verb.

NEGATIVE INDICATIVE PRESENT.

94. The negative indicative present is formed by adding the usual pronominal fragments to the infinitive. Thus:

SINGULAR.

1. చెప్పను	*cheppa-nu,*	I do not, or will not say.
2. చెప్పవు	*cheppa-vu,*	thou dost not say.
3. M. చెప్పడు	*cheppa-ḍu,*	he does not say.
F. & N. చెప్పదు	*cheppa-du,*	she or it does not say.

PLURAL.

1. చెప్పము	*cheppa-mu,*	they do not say.
2. చెప్పరు	*cheppa-ru,*	you do not say.
3. M. & F. చెప్పరు	*cheppa-ru,*	they do not say.
N. చెప్పవు	*cheppa-vu,*	they do not say.

NEGATIVE PAST TENSE.

95. The past tense is formed by adding లేదు *lédu,* the negative of the verb ఉండు *unḍu,* to be, to the infinitive, all the persons being the same. Thus: నేను చెప్పలేదు *nénu cheppa-lédu,* I did not say.

NEGATIVE IMPERATIVE.

96. The negative imperative is formed by adding to the infinitive the following words.

In the first person singular ఇయ్యక or ఇవ్వక *iyyaka* or *ivvaka,* the negative imperative of the verb ఇచ్చు *itstsu,* to give, the noun being in the objective case.

In the second person singular క *ka,* వద్దు *vaddu,* or బోకు *bóku.*

In the second person plural the same words with the addition of the plural or honorific affix అండి *anḍi.*

SINGULAR.

1.	నన్ను చెప్పనియ్యక	*nannu cheppa-(n)iyyaka,*	do not let me say, *lit.* do not give me to say.
2.	చెప్పక	*cheppa-ka,*	
	చెప్పవద్దు	*cheppa-vaddu,*	do not say.
	చెప్పబోకు	*cheppa-bóku,*	

PLURAL.

2.	చెప్పకండి	*cheppa-k(a)anḍi,*	
	చెప్పవద్దండి	*cheppa-vadd(u)anḍi,*	do not say.
	చెప్పబోకండి	*cheppa-bók(u)anḍi,*	

NEGATIVE PARTICIPLE.

97. The negative participle is formed by adding క *ka* to the infinitive. Thus: చెప్పక *cheppa-ka,* without saying.

NEGATIVE RELATIVE PARTICIPLE.

98. The negative relative participle is formed by adding ని *ni* to the infinitive. Thus: చెప్పని *cheppa-ni,* that does not say.

NEGATIVE VERBAL NOUN.

99. The negative verbal noun is formed by adding మి *mi* to the infinitive, or by using the negative participle in

క *ka* before పోవడము *pôvaḍamu* or ఉండడము *unḍaḍamu*, the verbal nouns of the verbs పోవు *pôvu*, to go, and ఉండు *unḍu*, to be. Thus: చెప్పమి *cheppa-mi*, the not saying, or చెప్పక పోవడము *cheppaka pôvaḍamu*, or చెప్పకవుండడము *cheppaka unḍaḍamu*, the going or being without saying.

Subjunctive Mood.

100. The subjunctive mood is formed by adding to the past participle, the affixes తే *té* or నట్టైతే *naṭṭaité*. Thus: చెప్పితే or చెప్పినట్టైతే *cheppi-té* or *cheppi-naṭṭaité*, if I say.

101. Other English tenses and moods, both in the affirmative and the negative, are formed by the use of the auxiliary verbs, and it will be convenient to state them in detail after the auxiliary verbs have been described.

(c.) *CONTRACTED FORM OF VERBS.*

102. Several pure Telugu verbs, such as the very common verbs, కొను *konu*, to take, to buy, విను *vinu*, to hear, తిను *tinu*, to eat, use short and easy contractions in the regular tenses. They contract the నుచు *nutsu* of the present into ంచు *ntsu*, and the నుతు *nutu* into ంటు *nṭu*, changing the soft palatal *t* into the hard cerebral *ṭ*. The principal forms of కొను *konu*, to buy, are appended.

103. కొను *konu*, to buy.

Present participle.

కొనుచు *konutsu*, } buying.
కొంచు *kontsu*, } buying.
కొంటు *konṭu*, } buying.

Past participle.

కొని *koni*, having bought.

PRESENT INDICATIVE.

Singular.

1. కొంచున్నాను *kontsu-nnánu*, I buy.
కొంటున్నాను *konṭu-nnánu*
కొంటాను *kont(u)-ánu*

2. కొంచున్నావు *kontsu-nnávu*, thou buyest.
కొంటున్నావు *konṭu-nnávu*
కొంటావు *konṭ(u)-ávu*

3. M. కొంచున్నాడు *kontsu-nnáḍu*, he buys.
కొంటున్నాడు *konṭu-nnáḍu*
కొంటాడు *konṭ(u)-áḍu*

F. & N. కొంచున్నది *kontsu-nnadi*, she or it buys.
కొంటున్నది *konṭ(u)-unnadi*

Plural.

1. కొంచున్నాము *kontsu-nnámu*, we buy.
కొంటున్నాము *konṭu-nnámu*
కొంటాము *konṭ(u)-ámu*

2. కొంచున్నారు *kontsu-nnáru,* ye buy.
కొంటున్నారు *konṭu-nnáru*
కొంటారు *konṭ(u)-áru*

3. M.&F. కొంచున్నారు *kontsu-nnáru,* they buy.
కొంటున్నారు *konṭu-nnáru*
కొంటారు *konṭ(u)-áru*
N. కొంచున్నవి *kontsu-nnavi*
కొంటున్నవి *konṭ(u)-unnavi*

Past Tense.

Formed from the past participle కొని *koni,* having bought, with the addition of న్నాను *nnánu,* &c., contracted from *konninnánu* to *konnánu.*

Singular.

1. కొన్నాను *konnánu,* I have bought.
కొంటిని *konṭini*

2. కొన్నావు *konnávu,* thou hast bought.
కొంటివి *konṭivi*

3. M. కొన్నాడు *konnáḍu,* he has bought.
కొనెను *konenu*
F. & N. కొన్నది *konnadi,* she or it has bought.
కొనెను *konenu*

Plural.

1. కొన్నాము	*konnámu,*	we have bought.
కొంటిమి	*konṭimi*	
2. కొన్నారు	*konnáru,*	ye have bought.
కొంటిరి	*konṭiri*	
3. M. & F. కొన్నారు	*konnáru,*	they have bought.
కొనిరి	*koniri*	
N. కొన్నివి	*konnivi,*	they have bought.
కొనెను	*konenu*	

AORIST.

Singular.

1 కొందును	*kondu-nu,*	I bought.
2. కొందువు	*konḍu-vu,*	thou boughtest.
3. కొనును	*konu-nu,*	he bought.

Plural.

1. కొందుము	*kondu-mu,*	we bought.
2. కొందురు	*kondu-ru,*	ye bought.
3. కొనును	*konu-nu,*	they bought.

IMPERATIVE MOOD.

2. Singular.	కొను	*konu,*	buy thou.
1. Plural.	కొందాము	*kondamu,*	let us buy.
2. Plural.	కొనండి	*konanḍi,*	buy ye.

Infinitive.

కొన *kona,* to buy.

Verbal Nouns.

కొనడము	*konaḍamu,*	the buying.
కొనుట	*konuṭa*	

Relative Participles.

Present.	కొంటున్న	*konṭunna,*	which buys.
Past.	కొన్న	*konna,*	which bought.
Indef.	కొనే	*koné,*	which bought.

Verbs with Other Terminations.

104. It was stated at the beginning of the section relating to the verbs that the variations in their formation were so few and so simple that there was practically only one conjugation in Telugu. Besides the class already described, there are groups of verbs ending in యు *yu* and in చు *tsu*; but the mode in which the tenses are formed is the same as that employed in the other verbs, that is, by affixing fragments of the personal pronouns; but they differ from the other verbs in the variations of the root itself, generally in the direction of euphony, and of clearness and simplicity of speech. Examples of both groups will now be given.

(ii.) Verbs ending in యు *yu*.

105. In most of the changes made when adding the pronominal affix, the root of verbs in యు *yu* generally

undergoes a change into సు *su*. Thus, the present participle in చేయు *chéyu*, to do, is చేస్తు *chéstu*, doing, the యు *yu* of the root being changed into సు *su*, and the affixed తు *tu* being joined on to it in a contracted form. The full form would naturally be చేసుతు *chésutu*, but, for the sake of euphony, it is contracted into the simpler form చేస్తు *chéstu*. The past participle is formed by changing the final *u* of the altered root into *i*. Thus, చేసి *chési*, having done. In the second form of the verbal noun and in the aorist, the root is similarly changed. Thus, చేసుట *chésuṭa*, doing, and చేసును *chésunu*, he did.

106. The full form is now given.

చేయు *chéyu*, to do.

Present participle చేస్తు *chéstu*, doing.

PRESENT INDICATIVE.

Singular.

1. చేస్తున్నాను	*chéstu-nnánu*,	I do.
చేస్తాను	*chéstánu*	
2. చేస్తున్నావు	*chéstu-nnávu*,	thou doest.
చేస్తావు	*chéstávu*	
3. M. చేస్తున్నాడు	*chéstu-nnáḍu*,	he does.
చేస్తాడు	*chéstáḍu*	
F. & N. చేస్తున్నది	*chéstu-nnadi*,	she or it does.

Plural.

1. చేస్తున్నాము	*chéstu-nnámu,*	we do.
చేస్తాము	*chéstámu*	
2. చేస్తున్నారు	*chéstu-nnáru,*	ye do.
చేస్తారు	*chéstáru*	
3. M. & F. చేస్తున్నారు	*chéstu-nnáru,*	they do.
చేస్తారు	*chéstáru*	
N. చేస్తున్నవి	*chéstu-nnavi,*	they do.

Past participle చేసి *chési,* having done.

PAST TENSE.

1. చేసినాను	*chési-nánu,*	I have done.
చేస్తిని	*chéstini*	
2. చేసినావు	*chési-návu,*	thou hast done.
చేస్తివి	*chéstivi*	
3. M. చేసినాడు	*chési-nádu,*	he has done.
చేసెను	*chésenu*	
F. & N. చేసినది	*chési-nadi,*	she or it has done.
చేసెను	*chésenu*	

Plural.

1. చేసినాము	*chési-námu,*	we have done.
చేస్తిమి	*chéstimi*	

2. చేసినారు	*chési-náru,*	ye have done.
చేస్తిరి	*chéstiri*	
3. M. & F. చేసినారు	*chési-náru,*	they have done.
చేసిరి	*chésiri*	
N. చేసినవి	*chési-navi,*	they have done.
చేసెను	*chésenu*	

AORIST.

Singular.

1. చేతును	*chétu-nu,*	I did.
2. చేతువు	*chétu-vu,*	thou didst.
3. చేసును	*chésu-nu,*	he, she, or it did.

Plural.

1. చేతుము	*chétu-mu,*	we did.
2. చేతురు	*chétu-ru,*	ye did.
3. M. & F. చేతురు	*chétu-ru,*	they did.
N. చేసును	*chésu-nu,*	they did.

INFINITIVE MOOD.

చేయ *chéya,* to do.

IMPERATIVE MOOD.

2.	Sing. చేయి	*chéy,*	do thou.
	చేయుము	*chéyumu*	
1.	Plur. చేతాము	*chétámu,*	let us do.
2.	చేయండి	*chéyanḍi,*	do ye.

The usual compounds with the auxiliary verb ఇచ్చు *itstsu*, to give, are also used. Thus : నన్ను చేయనియ్యి *nannu chéyaniyy*, let me do.

Relative Participles.

Present.	చేస్తున్న	*chéstu-nna,*	that does.
Past.	చేసిన	*chési-na,*	that did.
Indef.	చేసే	*chésé,*	that does, that did, or will do.

Verbal Nouns.

చేయడము	*chéya-ḍamu,*	the doing.
చేయుట	*chéyu-ṭa*	
చేసుట	*chésu-ṭa*	
చేసేది	*chésé-di*	

NEGATIVE FORM.

Present Indicative.

Singular.

1. చేయను	*chéya-nu,*	I do not.
2. చేయవు	*chéya-vu,*	thou dost not.
3. M. చేయడు	*chéya-ḍu,*	he does not.
F. & N. చేయదు	*chéya-du,*	she or it does not.

Plural.

1. చేయము	*chéya-mu,*	we do not.
2. చేయరు	*chéya-ru,*	ye do not.

3. M. & F. చేయరు *chéya-ru*, they do not.
N. చేయవు *chéya-vu*, they do not.

PAST TENSE.

చేయలేదు *chéya-lédu*, I did not.

PARTICIPLE.

చేయక *chéya-ka*, without doing.

RELATIVE PARTICIPLE.

చేయని *chéya-ni*, that does not, that will not do, or did not.

VERBAL NOUN.

చేయమి *chéya-mi*, the not doing.

IMPERATIVE.

2. Sing. చేయక *chéya-ka*, do not.
చేయవద్దు *chéya-vaddu*
చేయబోకు *chéya-bóku*.
2. Plur. చేయకండి *chéya-kanḍi*, do not ye.

VERBS IN యు *yu* OF THREE SYLLABLES.

107. Verbs of more than two syllables ending in యు *yu*, the penultimate being *i*, change the *i* into *u*, when followed by a syllable ending in *u*, and into *a* when followed by a syllable ending in *a*. Thus, జడియు *jaḍiyu*, to be afraid,

has జడుస్తు *jaḍustu* for its present participle, and జడుస్తాను *jaḍustánu*, as the present indicative. The infinitive is జడవ *jaḍava*; one of the verbal nouns, జడవడము *jaḍavaḍamu*; and the 2nd imperative plural, జడవండి *jaḍavanḍi*.

(iii.) Verbs ending in చు *tsu*.

108. As a general rule, verbs ending in చు *tsu* fall into two classes—(*a.*) those in two syllables, such as పెంచు *pentsu*, to rear, తూచు *tútsu*, to weigh, and దోచు *dótsu*, to rob, which are conjugated like ordinary verbs, and (*b.*) those of more than two syllables.

(*a.*) Dissyllabic Verbs in చు *tsu*.

109. The former, with a few exceptions, form the infinitive in the usual manner by changing the final *u* of the root into *a*, and they may change the చుదు *tsudu* of the aorist into తు *tu*, and the చుద *tsuda* of the affirmative imperative into త *ta*. If the root ends in a double చ *tsa*, the తు *tu* and త *ta* are also doubled. Thus, మెచ్చు *metstsu*, to approve, మెత్తురు *metturu*, they approved, మెత్తాము *mettámu*, let us approve.

(*b.*) Polysyllabic Verbs in చు *tsu*.

110. The great majority of these verbs are, however, of more than two syllables, and ం *n* precedes the final

చు *tsu.* These form the infinitive either in చ *tsa* or in ప *pa*, and in the aorist may take either తును *tunu* or స్తును *stụnu.* An example is appended.

111. అప్పగించు *appagintsu,* to deliver.

Present participle అప్పగిస్తు *appagistu,* delivering.

PRESENT INDICATIVE.

Singular.

1. అప్పగిస్తున్నాను *appagistu-nnánu,* I deliver.
అప్పగిస్తాను *appagistánu*
2. అప్పగిస్తున్నావు *appagistu-nnávu,* thou deliverest.
అప్పగిస్తావు *appagistávu*
3. M. అప్పగిస్తున్నాడు *appagistu-nnáḍu,* he delivers.
అప్పగిస్తాడు *appagistáḍu*
F. & N. అప్పగిస్తున్నది *appagistu-nnadi,* she or it delivers.

Plural.

1. అప్పగిస్తున్నాము *appagistu-nnámu,* we deliver.
అప్పగిస్తాము *appagistámu*
2. అప్పగిస్తున్నారు *appagistu-nnáru,* ye deliver.
అప్పగిస్తారు *appagistáru*
3. M. & F. అప్పగిస్తున్నారు *appagistu-nnáru,* they deliver.
అప్పగిస్తారు *appagistáru*
N. అప్పగిస్తున్నవి *appagistu-nnavi,* they deliver.

Past participle అప్పగించి, *appaginchi,* having delivered.

Past Tense.

Singular.

1. అప్పగించినాను	*appaginchi-nánu,*	I have delivered.
అప్పగిస్తిని	*appagistini*	
2. అప్పగించినావు	*appaginchi-návu,*	thou hast deli-
అప్పగిస్తివి	*appagistivi*	[vered.
3. M. అప్పగించినాడు	*appaginchi-nádu,*	he has delivered.
అప్పగించెను	*appaginchenu*	
F. & N. అప్పగించినది	*appaginchi-nadi,*	she or it has deli-
అప్పగించెను	*appaginchenu*	[vered.

Plural.

1. అప్పగించినాము	*appaginchi-námu,*	we have delivered.
అప్పగిస్తిమి	*appagistimi*	
2. అప్పగించినారు	*appaginchi-náru,*	ye have delivered.
అప్పగిస్తిరి	*appagistiri*	
3. M. & F. అప్పగించినారు	*appaginchi-náru,*	they have deli-
అప్పగించిరి	*appaginchiri*	[vered.
N. అప్పగించినవి	*appaginchi-navi,*	they have deli-
అప్పగించెను	*appaginchenu*	[vered.

Aorist.

Singular.

1. అప్పగింతును *appagintu-nu*, I delivered
2. అప్పగింతువు *appagintu-vu*, thou deliveredest.
3. M. F. & N. అప్పగించును *appagintsu-nu*, he, she, or it delivered.

Plural.

1. అప్పగింతుము *appagintu-mu*, we delivered.
2. అప్పగింతురు *appagintu-ru*, ye delivered.
3. M. & F. అప్పగింతురు *appagintu-ru*, they delivered.
   N. అప్పగించును *appagintsu-nu*, they delivered.

Infinitive.

అప్పగించ or అప్పగింప *appagintsa* or *appagimpa*, to deliver.

Imperative.

Singular.

2. అప్పగించు *appagintsu*, deliver thou.

Plural.

2. అప్పగించండి *appagintsaṇḍi*, deliver ye.

Relative Participles.

Present.

అప్పగిస్తున్న *appagistu-nna*, that delivers.

Past.

అప్పగించిన	*appaginchi-na,*	that delivered.

Indefinite.

అప్పగించే	*appaginché,*	that delivered.

VERBAL NOUNS.

అప్పగించడము	*appagintsa-ḍamu,*	the delivering.
అప్పగించుట	*appagintsu-ṭa*	
అప్పగించేది	*appaginché-di*	

112. Some verbs of three syllables which have no ం *n* before the final చు *tsu,* form the infinitive in వ *va,* as కరచు *karatsu,* to bite, కరవ *karava*; నిలుచు *nilutsu,* to stand, నిలవ *nilava*; పిలుచు *pilutsu,* to call, పిలవ *pilava;* while others form the infinitive both in చ *tsa* and in వ *va,* as ఈడుచు *íḍutsu,* to pull, నలుచు *nalutsu,* to crush.

(iv.) PECULIAR VERBS.

113. The following verbs in very common use form the infinitive and the imperative in a manner peculiar to themselves.

Verbs.	*Infinitive.*	*Imperative.*
ఇచ్చు *itstsu,* to give	ఇవ్వ or ఇయ్య *ivva* or *iyya,*	ఇయ్య *iyy*
వచ్చు *vatstsu,* to come	రా *rá*	రా *rá*
తెచ్చు *tetstsu,* to bring	తే *té*	తే *té*

నొచ్చు *notstsu*,	to hurt	నొవ్వ *novva*	నొవ్వు *novvu*
చచ్చు *tsatstsu*,	to die	చావ *tsáva*	చావు *tsávu*
చూచు *tsútsu*,	to see.	చూడ *tsúḍa*	చూడు *tsúḍu*

(v.) Auxiliary Verbs.

114. A vast variety of subtle and delicate phases of speech can be obtained by the skilful use of the auxiliary verbs. The ordinary moods of desire, entreaty, subjection, and command are thus expressed; and the use of participles or infinitives, in conjunction with other verbs, and especially with the auxiliary verbs, makes various combinations which, in languages belonging to other families, particularly the Áryan, are made by the frequent employment of prepositions. Some of these forms will presently be shown; but it is necessary first to give some account of the chief auxiliary verbs. These are ఉండు *unḍu*, to be, అవు *au*, to become, కలుగు *kalugu*, to exist or to be, and వలయు *valayu*, to wish. నేరు *néru*, to be able, చాలు *tsálu*, to suffice, వచ్చు *vatstsu*, to come, పోవు *póvu*, to go, ఇచ్చు *itstsu*, to give, తగు *tagu*, to fit, are also used as auxiliary verbs.

115. Most of these verbs are so exceedingly useful, and occur so frequently in everyday speech, that their principal parts are now given, and it will then be shown how intimately they are connected with the formation in Telugu of the usual compound moods and tenses of the English verbs.

(a.) *FIRST AUXILIARY VERB.*

116. ఉండు *undu*, to be.

ROOT ఉండు *undu*.

Present Participle ఉంటు *untu*, being.

PRESENT INDICATIVE.

Singular.

1. ఉంటున్నాను	*untu-nnánu,*	I am.
ఉంటాను	*untánu*	
2. ఉంటున్నావు	*untu-nnávu,*	thou art.
3. M. ఉంటున్నాడు	*untu-nnádu,*	he is.
F. & N. ఉంటున్నది	*untu-nnadi,*	she or it is.

Plural.

1. ఉంటున్నాము	*untu-nnámu,*	we are.
2. ఉంటున్నారు	*untu-nnáru,*	ye are.
3. M. & F. ఉంటున్నారు	*untu-nnáru,*	they are.
N. ఉంటున్నవి	*untu-nnavi,*	they are.

Past Participle ఉండి *undi*, having been.

PAST TENSE.

1. ఉండినాను	*undi-nánu,*	I have been.
ఉంటిని	*untini*	
2. ఉండినావు	*undi-návu,*	thou hast been.
ఉంటివి	*untivi*	

3. M. ఉండినాడు	*undi-nádu,*	he has been.
ఉండెను	*undenu*	
F. & N. ఉండినది	*undi-nadi,*	she or it has been.
ఉండెను	*undenu*	

Plural.

1. ఉండినాము	*undi-námu,*	we have been.
ఉంటిమి	*untimi*	
2. ఉండినారు	*undi-náru,*	ye have been.
ఉంటిరి	*untiri*	
3. M. & F. ఉండినారు	*undi-náru,*	they have been.
ఉండిరి	*undiri*	
N. ఉండినవి	*undi-navi,*	they have been.
ఉండెను	*undenu*	

117. There is another form of the past tense, which is constantly used for the present. In fact, it is the real present, and is the root and groundwork of the formation of the present tense in all varieties of the verb. It is evidently formed from ఉన్న *unna,* the contracted form of the past relative participle, with the usual pronominal affixes. It is as follows:

PAST TENSE.

Singular.

1. ఉన్నాను	*unnánu,*	I was.
2. ఉన్నావు	*unnávu,*	thou wast.
3. M. ఉన్నాడు	*unnádu,*	he was.
F. & N. ఉన్నది	*unnadi,*	she or it was.

Plural.

1. ఉన్నాము	*unnámu,*	we were.
2. ఉన్నారు	*unnáru,*	ye were.
3. M. & F. ఉన్నారు	*unnáru,*	they were.
N. ఉన్నవి	*unnavi,*	they were.

AORIST.

Singular.

1. ఉందును	*undu-nu,*	I was.
2. ఉందువు	*undu-vu,*	thou wast.
3. ఉండును	*unḍu-nu,*	he, she, or it was.

Plural.

1. ఉందుము	*undu-mu,*	we were.
2. ఉందురు	*undu-ru,*	ye were.
3. M. & F. ఉండురు	*undu-ru,*	they were.
N. ఉండును	*unḍu-nu*	

118. INFINITIVE ఉండ *unḍa,* to be.

PRESENT RELATIVE PART.	ఉంటున్న	*unṭunna,*	that is.
PAST RELATIVE PART.	ఉండిన	*unḍina,*	that was.
Contracted form	ఉన్న	*unna,*	
INDEFINITE RELATIVE PART.	ఉండే	*unḍé,*	that is or was.
VERBAL NOUNS.	ఉండడము	*unḍa-ḍamu,*	being.
	ఉండుట	*unḍu-ṭa,*	
	ఉండేది	*unḍé-di*	

119. NEGATIVE FORM.

PARTICIPLE.	ఉండక	*unḍaka,*	not being.
RELATIVE PART.	ఉండని	*unḍani,*	that was not.

AORIST INDICATIVE.

There are two forms of the aorist indicative negative. The first is formed in the regular way by additions to the infinitive, and it generally has a future sense, and signifies 'not remaining'; and the second is formed by the usual additions to an entirely different root, namely లే *lé.* Thus:

Singular.

1.	ఉండను	*unḍa-nu,*	I will not be.
2.	ఉండవు	*unḍa-vu,*	thou wilt not be.
3.	M. ఉండడు	*unḍa-ḍu,*	he will not be.
	F. & N. ఉండదు	*unḍa-du,*	she or it will not be.

Plural.

1.	ఉండము	*unḍa-mu,*	we will not be.
2.	ఉండరు	*unḍa-ru,*	ye will not be.
3.	M. & F. ఉండరు	*unḍa-ru,*	they will not be.
	N. ఉండవు	*unḍa-vu,*	they will not be.

SECOND FORM.

Singular.

1.	లేను	*lénu,*	I was not.
2.	లేవు	*lévu,*	thou wast not.

3. M. లేడు	*léḍu,*	he was not.
F. &. N. లేదు	*lédu,*	she or it was not.

Plural.

1. లేము	*lému,*	we were not.
2. లేరు	*léru,*	ye were not.
3. M. &. F లేరు	*léru,*	they were not.
N. లేవు	*lévu,*	they were not.

IMPERATIVE.

2. Sing. ఉండకు	*unḍa-ku,*	be not thou.
2. Plu. ఉండకండి	*unḍa-kanḍi,*	be not ye.

120. (*b.*) *SECOND AUXILIARY VERB.*

అవు *au,* to become.

PRESENT PARTICIPLE	అవుతు	*autu,*	becoming.
PAST PARTICIPLE	అయి	*ai,*	having become.
INFINITIVE	కా	*ká,*	to become.

PRESENT INDICATIVE.

Singular.

1. అవుతాను	*autánu,*	I become.
2. అవుతావు	*autávu,*	thou becomest.
3. M. అవుతాడు	*autáḍu,*	he becomes.
F. & N. అవుతున్నది	*autunnadi,*	she or it becomes.

Plural.

1.	అవుతాము	*autámu,*	we become.
2.	అవుతారు	*autáru,*	ye become.
3.	M. & F. అవుతారు	*autáru,*	they become.
	N. అవుతున్నవి	*autunnavi,*	they become.

PAST TENSE.

Singular.

1.	అయినాను	*ainánu,*	I have become.
	or అయితిని	*aitini*	
2.	అయినావు	*ainávu,*	thou hast become.
	అయితివి	*aitivi*	
3.	M. అయినాడు	*ainádu,*	he has become.
	ఆయెను	*áyenu*	
	F. & N. అయినది	*ainadi,*	she or it has become.
	ఆయెను	*áyenu*	

Plural.

1.	అయినాము	*ainámu,*	we have become.
	అయితిమి	*aitimi*	
2.	అయినారు	*ainárú,*	ye have become.
	అయితిరి	*aitiri*	
3.	M. & F. అయినారు	*ainárú,*	they have become.
	అయిరి	*airi*	

N. అయినవి	*ainavi,*	they have become.
ఆయెను	*áyenu*	

The Aorist.

Singular.

1. అవుదును	*audunu,*	I became.
2. అవుదువు	*auduvu,*	thou becamest.
3. అవును	*aunu,*	he, she, or it became.

Plural.

1. అవుదుము	*audumu,*	we became.
2. అవుదురు	*auduru,*	ye became.
3. M. & F. అవుదురు	*auduru,*	they became.
N. అవును	*aunu,*	they became.

Imperative.

2. Singular	కా	*ká,*	become thou.
2. Plural	కండి	*kanḍi,*	become ye.

Relative Participles.

Present	అవుతున్న	*autunna,*	that becomes.
Past	అయిన	*aina,*	that became.
Indefinite	అయ్యే	*ayyé,*	that becomes or became.

VERBAL NOUNS.

కావడము	*kávaḍamu,*	becoming.
అవుట	*auṭa*	
అయ్యేది	*ayyédi*	

NEGATIVE FORM.

Aorist Singular.

1. కాను	*kánu,*	I do not become.
2. కావు	*kávu,*	thou dost not become.
3. M. కాడు	*káḍu,*	he does not become.
F. & N. కాదు	*kádu,*	she or it does not become.

Plural.

1. కాము	*kámu,*	we do not become.
2. కారు	*káru,*	ye do not become.
3. M. & F. కారు	*káru,*	they do not become.
N. కావు	*kávu,*	they do not become.

Imperative.

2. Sing. కాక	*káka,*	become not thou.
2. Plur. కాకండి	*kákanḍi,*	become not ye.

VERBAL PARTICIPLE.

కాక	*káka,*	without becoming.

Relative Participle.

కాని	*káni,*	that does not become.

Verbal Noun.

కామి	*kámi,*	the not becoming.

121. (c). *THIRD AUXILIARY VERB*

కలుగు *kalugu,* to be, to happen.

This verb is very irregular and defective. There is no present indicative.

Infinitive	కలగ	*kalaga,*	to be.
Pres. Part.	కలుగుతు	*kalugutu,*	being.
Past. Part.	కలిగి	*kaligi,*	having been.

Past Indicative.

కలిగినాను	*kaliginánu,*	I was.
or కలిగితిని	*kaligitini,* &c.	

The Aorist Indicative.

Singular.

1. కలుగుదును	*kalugudunu,*	I was.

The commoner form, however, is:

1. కలను	*kalanu,*	I was.
2. కలవు	*kalavu,*	thou wast.
3. M. కలడు	*kaladu,*	he was.
F. & N. కలదు	*kaladu,*	she or it was.
Cont. కద్దు	*kaddu*	

Plural.

1. కలము	*kalamu,*	we were.
2. కలరు	*kalaru,*	ye were.
3. M. & F. కలరు	*kalaru,*	they were.
N. కలవు	*kalavu,*	they were.
Relative Part. కల	*kala,*	that was.
Negative Part. కలగని	*kalagani,*	that was not.

122. (*d.*) THE AUXILIARY VERB

వలయు *valayu,* to wish.

This is another very defective, but very common and useful auxiliary verb. Only the most useful parts of it are given.

Past participle	వలసి or వలశి	*valasi* or *valaṣi.*
Rel. participle	వలసిన,	*valasina.*

PAST TENSE.

3. Sing. N. వలసినది *valasinadi*, it must, it is to be wished.

వలెను *valenu*

3. Plural N. వలసినవి *valasinavi*, they must.

AORIST.

3. Sing. N. వలయును *valayunu*, it must.

3. Neg. Sing. N. వలదు *valadu*, it must not.

Contracted వద్దు *vaddu*

23. (*e.*) *THE AUXILIARY VERB*

నేరు *néru*, to be able, can.

AORIST INDICATIVE.

Singular.

1. నేర్తును *nértunu*, I can.
2. నేర్తువు *nértuvu*, thou canst.
3. నేర్చును *nértsunu*, he, she, or it can.

Plural.

నేర్తుము *nértumu*, we can.

నేర్తురు *nérturu*, ye can.

M. and F. నేర్తురు *nérturu*, they can.

N. నేర్చును *nértsunu*, they can.

NEGATIVE AORIST.

Singular.

1. నేరను	*néranu,*	I cannot.
2. నేరవు	*néravu,*	thou canst not.
3. M. నేరడు	*néraḍu,*	he cannot.
F. & N. నేరదు	*néradu,*	she or it cannot.

Plural.

1. నేరము	*néramu,*	we cannot.
2. నేరరు	*néraru,*	ye cannot.
3. M. & F. నేరరు	*néraru*	they cannot.
N. నేరవు	*néravu,*	they cannot.

124. (*f.*) *THE AUXILIARY VERB*

చాలు *tsálu,* to suffice.

The aorist of this root, both affirmative and negative, is often used as an auxiliary verb in the sense of 'can' or 'cannot.'

AORIST.

Affirmative Singular.

1. చాలుదును	*tsáludunu,*	I can.
2. చాలుదువు	*tsáluduvu,*	thou canst.
3. చాలును	*tsálunu,*	he, she, or it can.

Plural.

1. చాలుదుము *tsáludumu,* we can.
2. చాలుదురు *tsáluduru,* ye can.
3. M. & F. చాలుదురు *tsáluduru,* they can.
   N. చాలును *tsálunu,* they can.

Negative Singular.

1. చాలను *tsálanu,* I cannot.
2. చాలవు *tsálavu,* thou canst not.
3. M. చాలడు *tsálaḍu,* he cannot.
   F. & N. చాలదు *tsáladu,* she or it cannot.

Plural.

1. చాలము *tsálamu,* we cannot.
2. చాలరు *tsálaru,* ye cannot.
3. M. & F. చాలరు *tsálaru,* they cannot.
   N. చాలవు *tsálavu,* they cannot.

125. The verbs వచ్చు *vatstsu,* to come, and పోవు *póvu,* to go, are also used as auxiliary verbs; and, as they are very irregular, not in the way in which the pronominal affixes are added, but in the variations in the formation of their roots, and as they are in common, every day use, the formation of their principal tenses are given.

126. (*g.*) వచ్చు *vatstsu*, to come.

The present participle is a contracted form of what would naturally be the regular formation.

Present participle వస్తు *vastu*, coming.

Present Indicative.

Singular.

1. వస్తున్నాను	*vastunnánu*,	I come.
or వస్తాను	*vastánu*	
2. వస్తున్నావు	*vastunnávu*,	thou comest.
3. M. వస్తున్నాడు	*vastunnáḍu*,	he comes.
F. & N. వస్తున్నది	*vastunnadi*,	she or it comes.

Plural.

1. వస్తున్నాము	*vastunnámu*,	we come.
2. వస్తున్నారు	*vastunnáru*,	ye come.
3. M. & F. వస్తున్నారు	*vastunnáru*,	they come.
N. వస్తున్నవి	*vastunnavi*,	they come.
Past participle. వచ్చి	*vachchi*,	having come.

Past Tense.

Singular.

1. వచ్చినాను	*vachchinánu*,	I have come.
2. వచ్చినావు	*vachchinávu*,	thou hast come.

3. M. వచ్చినాడు	*vachchináḍu,*	he has come.
F. & N. వచ్చినది	*vachchinadi,*	she or it has come.
M. F. & N. వచ్చెను	*vachchenu*	

Plural.

1. వచ్చినాము	*vachchinámu,*	we have come.
2. వచ్చినారు	*vachchináru,*	ye have come.
3. M. & F. వచ్చినారు	*vachchináru,*	they have come.
N. వచ్చినవి	*vachchinavi,*	they have come.
వచ్చెను	*vachchenu*	

The aorist is formed by adding the pronominal affixes to a changed form of the root, except in the third person, where it is formed in the usual way.

The Aorist.

Singular.

1. వత్తును	*vattunu,*	I came.
2. వత్తువు	*vattuvu,*	thou camest.
3. వచ్చును	*vatstsunu,*	he, she, or it came.

Plural.

1. వత్తుము	*vattumu,*	we came.
2. వత్తురు	*vatturu,*	ye came.
3. M. & F. వత్తురు	*vatturu,*	they came
N. వచ్చును	*vatstsunu,*	they came.

IMPERATIVE MOOD.

2. Sing. రా or రమ్ము		*rá* or *rammu*,	come thou.
2. Plur. రండి		*randi*,	come ye.
Infinitive	రా	*rá*,	to come.
Present rel. part.	వస్తున్న	*vastunna*,	that comes.
Past rel. part.	వచ్చిన	*vachchina*,	that has came.
Ind. rel. part.	వచ్చే	*vachché*,	that came.
Verbal Nouns.	రావడము	*rávadamu*	the coming.
	వచ్చుట	*vatstsuta*	
	వచ్చేది	*vachchédi*	

THE NEGATIVE VERB.

PRESENT.

Singular.

1. రాను	*ránu*,	I come not, or do not come.
2. రావు	*rávu*,	thou comest not.
3. M. రాడు	*rádu*,	he comes not.
F. & N. రాదు	*rádu*,	she or it comes not.

Plural.

1. రాము	*rámu*,	we come not.
2. రారు	*ráru*,	ye come not.
3. M. & F. రారు	*ráru*,	they come not.
N. రావు	*rávu*,	they come not.

Imperative Mood.

2. Sing. రాక	*ráka,*	come not thou.
2. Plur. రాకండి	*rákanḍi,*	come not ye.

127. (*h.*) పోవు *póvu,* to go.

In the greater part of the Telugu country this verb is almost entirely used for auxiliary purposes, the word in ordinary use for 'to go' being వెళ్లు *veḷlu.*

The present participle is a contracted form of what might be expected to be its full formation; that is పోతు *pótu* instead of పోవుతు *póvutu.*

Present Participle పోతు	*pótu,*	going.

Present Indicative.

Singular.

1. పోతున్నాను	*pótunnánu,*	I go.
2. పోతున్నావు	*pótunnávu,*	thou goest.
3. M. పోతున్నాడు	*pótunnáḍu,*	he goes.
F. & N. పోతున్నది	*pótunnadi,*	she or it goes.

Plural.

1. పోతున్నాము	*pótunnámu,*	we go.
2. పోతున్నారు	*pótunnáru,*	ye go.
3. M. & F. పోతున్నారు	*pótunnáru,*	they go.
N. పోతున్నవి	*pótunnavi,*	they go.

The past participle is most irregular; but is probably a popular contraction of what a regular formation would be, or what it really was in former times.

Past Participle	పోయి	*póy,*	having gone.

PAST TENSE.

Singular.

1.	పోయినాను	*póynánu,*	I have gone.
	or పోతిని	*pótini*	
2.	పోయినావు	*póynávu,*	thou hast gone.
3.	M. పోయినాడు	*póynáḍu,*	he has gone.
	F. & N. పోయినది	*póynadi,*	she or it has gone.
	M. F. & N. పోయెను	*póyenu,*	he, she, or it has gone.

Plural.

1.	పోయినాము	*póynámu,*	we have gone.
2.	పోయినారు	*póynáru,*	ye have gone.
3.	M. & F పోయినారు	*póynáru,*	they have gone.
	N. పోయినవి	*póynavi,*	they have gone.
	M. F. & N. పోయెను	*póyenu,*	they have gone.

THE AORIST.

The aorist is still more irregular, the pronominal affixes being added to no known part of the verb or root.

Singular.

1. పోదును	*pódunu,*	I went.
2. పోదువు	*póduvu,*	thou wentest.

Plural.

1. పోదుము	*pódumu,*	we went.
2. పోదురు	*póduru,*	ye went.
3. M. & F. పోదురు	*póduru,*	they went.

IMPERATIVE MOOD.

2. Sing.	పో	*pó,*	go thou.
1. Plur.	పోదాము	*pódámu,*	let us go.
2. Plur.	పొండి	*pondi,*	go ye.

Infinitive	పో	*pó,*	to go.
Present rel. part.	పోతున్న	*pótunna,*	that goes.
Past rel. part.	పోయిన	*póyna,*	that has gone.
Ind. rel. part.	పోయ్యే	*póyyé,*	that went.
Verbal Nouns	పోవడము	*póvaḍamu,*	the going.
	పోవుట	*póvuṭa,*	
	పొయ్యేది	*poyyédi,*	

The Negative Verb.

Aorist Singular.

1. పోను *pónu,* I went not.
2. పోవు *póvu,* thou wentest not.
3. M. పోడు *póḍu,* he went not.
   F. & N. పోదు *pódu,* she or it went not.

Plural.

1. పోము *pómu,* we went not.
2. పోరు *póru,* ye went not.
3. M. & F. పోరు *póru,* they went not.
   N. పోవు *póvu,* they went not.

Imperative Mood.

2. Sing. పోక *póka,* go not thou.
2. Plur. పోకండి *pókanḍi,* go not ye.

(vi.) Compound Tenses.

128. Some of the principal forms of the auxiliary verbs having been given, the way has been prepared for explaining the mode in which the usual compound tenses of the English verb can appropriately be rendered into Telugu. The auxiliaries can be used with verbs of all kinds irrespective of their terminations, the verbs in యు *yu* and చు *tsu* being treated in exactly the same way as the other

verbs. The most convenient arrangement will be to take the verb which has already been given as an example, and to show how it is affected by the use of the auxiliary verbs. The root taken for an example is చెప్పు *cheppu,* to say.

129. The progressive present, or the present imperfect, is expressed by lengthening the final *u* of the present participle, and adding to it the past tense of ఉండు *unḍu,* to be, used in a present sense. Thus: చెప్పుతూఉన్నాను *chepputú unnánu,* I am saying. In this instance, and in all the following instances, the affixed auxiliary verb is conjugated in all its persons. Thus:—చెప్పుతూఉన్నావు *chepputú unnávu,* thou art saying, &c.

130. The imperfect or past imperfect is expressed, in a similar manner, by adding the past tense of ఉండు *unḍu,* to be, to the present participle. Thus: చెప్పుతూఉంటిని *chepputú unṭini,* I was saying.

131. The pluperfect is expressed by adding the past tense of ఉండు *unḍu,* to the past tense of the verb which it is helping. Thus: చెప్పిఉన్నాను *cheppi unnánu,* I had said.

132. The ordinary way of forming the present subjunctive is by adding తే *té* to the past participle. Thus: చెప్పితే *cheppité,* if I say. A longer form, but equally common, is by adding ట్టైతే *ṭṭaité,* to the past relative participle. Thus: చెప్పినట్టైతే *cheppinaṭṭaité,* if I say.

133. The pluperfect subjunctive is expressed by adding ఉంటే *unṭé,* the present subjunctive of ఉండు *unḍu,* to be, to the past participle. Thus: చెప్పియుంటే *cheppi-unṭé,* if I had said.

134. The Potential Mood is expressed in several ways, indicating various degrees and delicate shades of meaning which are difficult to define. Several auxiliary verbs are employed for this purpose, and are interchangeable in ordinary conversation. Thus the difference between "I am able" and "I can," in English, is very slight; and, similarly, in Telugu, నేరు *néru,* to be able, and వచ్చు *vatstsu,* to come, when used as auxiliary verbs, are very much alike; but one means rather ability to do anything, and the other, readiness. The aorist of the auxiliary is added to the infinitive of the verb it assists. Thus:

చెప్పగలను	*cheppa-galanu,*	I can say.
చెప్పగలుదును	*cheppa-galudunu,*	
చెప్పవచ్చును	*cheppa-vatstsunu,*	
చెప్పచాలుదును	*cheppa-tsáludunu,*	
చెప్ప నేర్తును	*cheppa-nértunu.*	

135. The negative aorist is used to express the negation, added, like the affirmative, to the infinitive mood. Thus: చెప్పచాలను *cheppa-tsálanu,* I cannot say.

136. The present potential, "must," is represented by వలసినది *valasinadi,* or వలెను *valenu,* being joined to the infinitive of a verb. Thus: చెప్పవలసినది *cheppa-valasinadi,* or

చెప్పవలెను *cheppa-valenu,* I must say. చెప్పరాదు *cheppa-rádu,* I must not say.

137. చెప్పలేను *cheppa-lénu* is also the negative of the potential mood, while చెప్పలేదు *cheppa-lédu,* I did not, is the negative of the past indicative. A careful distinction between these two forms should be clearly apprehended, and constantly borne in mind. లేను *lénu,* I cannot, is used in all the persons, being conjugated throughout, whereas లేదు *lédu,* added to a verb in the sense of "did not" remains the same in all the persons.

138. In the past tense of the potential mood, చెప్పగలిగితిని *cheppa-galigitini* represents, I should say, and చెప్పుదును *cheppudunu,* I would say, while చెప్పలేకపోతిని *cheppa-léka-pótini* means, I could not say, literally, I have gone without saying.

139. The English auxiliary verb "ought" is represented by the past tense of a similar verb in Telugu being added to the infinitive, namely తగినది *taginadi,* the third person singular past of తగు *tagu,* to be. Thus: నేను చెప్పతగినది *nénu cheppa-taginadi,* I ought to say. The negative is formed by adding to the infinitive of any verb కూడదు *kúḍadu,* being the third person singular negative aorist of the verb కూడు *kúḍu,* to be possible, to agree.

140. The pluperfect potential is expressed by adding

to the past participle of a verb the aorist of the auxiliary verb, వుండు *undu*, to be. Thus: నేను చెప్పివుందును *nénu cheppi-undunu*, I would have said.

141. A strong mode of expressing impossibility is by appending the phrase వల్లకాదు *valla kádu*, it is not possible, to the infinitive. Thus: చెప్పవల్లకాదు *cheppavalla-kádu*, it is impossible to say.

(vii.) Passive Voice.

142. As a general rule, there is really no passive voice in the Dravidian languages, that form of construction being contrary to the genius of this family of languages. In ordinary conversation the sense is either conveyed by putting an assertion in the direct and active form, or by a periphrasis. Thus, such a phrase as "those words were spoken by him" would be rendered in conversation by the more direct form, "he spoke those words." The passive can, however, be expressed by adding the verb పడు *paḍu*, to fall or to suffer, to the infinitive of any transitive verb. పడు *paḍu* is thus used as an auxiliary verb, and it alone is conjugated, the verb which it modifies remaining throughout in the infinitive. The initial ప *pa* is changed into బ *ba*, the infinitive being a *druta* word. This change is commonly used even in the most familiar talk. An example of the passive voice is given below, the transitive verb పంపు *pampu*, to send, being selected for the purpose.

పంపబడు *pampa-baḍu,* to be sent.

Present part. పంపబడుతు *pampa-baḍutu,* being sent.

Present Tense.

Singular.

1.	పంపబడుతున్నాను	*pampa-baḍutunnánu,*	I am sent.
2.	పంపబడుతున్నావు	*pampa-baḍutunnávu,*	thou art sent.
3. M.	పంపబడుతున్నాడు	*pampa-baḍutunnáḍu,*	he is sent.
F. & N.	పంపబడుతున్నది	*pampa-baḍutunnadi,*	she or it is sent.

Plural.

1.	పంపబడుతున్నాము	*pampa-baḍutunnámu,*	we are sent.
2.	పంపబడుతున్నారు	*pampa-baḍutunnáru,*	ye are sent.
3. M. & F.	పంపబడుతున్నారు	*pampa-baḍutunnáru,*	they are sent.
N.	పంపబడుతున్నవి	*pampa-baḍutunnavi,*	they are sent.
Past part.	పంపబడి	*pampa-baḍi,*	having been sent.

Past Tense.

The past tense is formed regularly, as పంపబడినాను or పంపబడితిని *pampa-baḍi-nánu* or *pampa-baḍi-tini,* and it has also a contracted form which is most commonly used, namely, పంపబడ్డాను *pampa-baḍḍánu.*

Singular.

1.	పంపబడ్డాను	*pampa-baḍḍánu,*	I have been sent.
2.	పంపబడ్డావు	*pampa-baḍḍávu,*	thou hast been sent.

3. M. పంపబడ్డాడు	*pampa-baḍḍáḍu,*	he has been sent.
F. & N. పంపబడ్డది	*pampa-baḍḍadi,*	she or it has been sent.

Plural.

1. పంపబడ్డాము	*pampa-baḍḍámu,*	we have been sent.
2. పంపబడ్డారు	*pampa-baḍḍáru,*	ye have been sent.
3. M. & F. పంపబడ్డారు	*pampa-baḍḍáru,*	they have been sent.
N. పంపబడ్డవి	*pampa-baḍḍavi,*	they have been sent.

THE AORIST.

Singular.

1. పంపబడుదును	*pampa-baḍudunu,*	I was sent.
2. పంపబడుదువు	*pampa-baḍuduvu,*	thou wast sent.
3. పంపబడును	*pampa-baḍunu,*	he, she, or it was sent.

Infinitive	పంపబడ	*pampa-baḍa,*	to be sent.
Pres. rel. part.	పంపబడుతున్న	*pampa-baḍutunna,*	that is sent.
Past rel. part.	పంపబడ్డ	*pampa-baḍḍa,*	that has been sent.
Ind. rel. part.	పంపబడే	*pampa-baḍé,*	that was sent.
Verbal noun	పంపబడడము	*pampa-baḍaḍamu,*	the being sent.

Negative Form.

Singular.

1.	పంపబడను	*pampa-baḍanu,*	I was not sent.
2.	పంపబడవు	*pampa-baḍavu,*	thou wast not sent.
3.	M. పంపబడడు	*pampa-baḍaḍu,*	he was not sent.
	F. & N. పంపబడదు	*pampa-baḍadu,*	she or it was not sent.

Plural.

1.	పంపబడము	*pampa-baḍamu,*	we were not sent.
2.	పంపబడరు	*pampa-baḍaru,*	ye were not sent.
3.	M. & F. పంపబడరు	*pampa-baḍaru,*	they were not sent.
	N. పంపబడవు	*pampa-baḍavu,*	they were not sent.

(viii.) Reflective Verbs.

143. Verbs can be converted into a reflective form, that is, they can be used in the middle voice, by adding కొను *konu,* to buy, to the root. Each verb thus altered is conjugated like కొను *konu,* in all its parts, with the exception of the infinitive mood and of the first person singular imperative, which in కొను *konu,* to buy, are respectively కొన *kona,* and కొను *konu,* but in the auxiliary form both

become కో *kó*. Thus: చెప్పు *cheppu*, to say or speak, becomes చెప్పుకొను *cheppu-konu*, to speak for oneself.

144. చెప్పుకొను *cheppu-konu*, to speak for oneself.

Infinitive	చెప్పుకో	*cheppu-kó*,	to speak for oneself.
Pres. part.	చెప్పుకొంటు	*cheppu-konṭu*,	speaking for oneself.
Past part.	చెప్పుకొని	*cheppu-koni*,	having spoken, &c.
Pres. Ind.	చెప్పుకొంటున్నాను	*cheppu-konṭunnánu*,	I speak, &c.
Past tense	చెప్పుకొన్నాను	*cheppu-konnánu*,	I have spoken, &c.
Aorist	చెప్పుకొందును	*cheppu-kondunu*,	I spoke, &c.
Imperative	చెప్పుకో	*cheppu-kó*,	speak, &c.
Pres. rel. part.	చెప్పుకొంటున్న	*cheppu-konṭunna*,	that speaks, &c.
Past rel. part.	చెప్పుకొన్న	*cheppu-konna*,	that has spoken, &c.
Ind. rel. part.	చెప్పుకొనే	*cheppu-koné*,	that spoke, &c.

145. Verbs whose roots end in యు *yu* change this syllable into సు *su* before receiving the addition of కొను *konu*. Thus: చేయు *chéyu*, to do, as a reflective verb, becomes చేసుకొను *chésu-konu*, to do or act for oneself.

146. In verbs consisting of two short syllables the initial *ko* of కొను *konu*, is generally doubled. Thus: కొను కొన్కొను *konu-kkonu*, to buy for oneself.

147. Certain verbs ending in గు *gu*, drop the final గు *gu* in composition, and the initial *k*, of కొను *konu*, is doubled. Thus: అడుగు *aḍugu*, to ask, becomes అడుక్కొను *aḍu-kkonu*, to beg, or to ask for oneself.

(ix.) Causal Verbs.

148. As a general rule, all verbs, except those ending in చు *tsu*, can be converted into causals by changing the final *u* of the root into *intsu*. Thus: చెప్పు *cheppu*, to say, చెప్పించు *cheppintsu*, to cause to speak; అంటు *anṭu*, to touch, అంటించు *anṭintsu*, to cause to touch; చేయు *chéyu*, to do, చేయించు *chéyintsu*, to cause to be done.

149. Verbs ending in చు *tsu* generally form the causal by changing the final *tsu* of the root into పించు *pintsu*, and చ్చు *tsṭsu* into ప్పించు *ppintsu*; and, if the penultimate is an *u*, changing it, for the sake of euphony, into *i*. Thus: తూచు *tútsu*, to weigh, తూపించు *túpintsu*, to cause to weigh; యిచ్చు *itstsu*, to give, యిప్పించు *ippintsu*, to cause to give; పిలుచు *pilutsu*, to call, పిలిపించు *pilipintsu*, to cause to be called, or to send for.

150. There are exceptions to the above general rule, which can best be learned in daily practice. Thus:

వచ్చు	*vatstsu,*	to come	రప్పించు	*rappintsu,* to cause to come, or to fetch.
కాగు	*kágu,*	to burn	కాచు	*kátsu,* to boil.
లేచు	*létsu,*	to rise	లేపు	*lépu,* to raise.

Causal verbs ending in చు *tsu* are conjugated like other verbs of the same termination.

151. Many verbs are employed as auxiliaries either to add emphasis to an assertion, or to give the additional force which, in other languages, as English or Greek, would be imparted by prepositions, either separately or in composition. వేయు *véyu,* to throw, is frequently used in this manner. Thus: కోసివేయు *kósi-véyu,* to cut off; పారివేయు *pári-véyu,* to throw away; తీసివేయు *tísi-véyu,* to draw out. పడ *paḍa,* the infinitive of పడు *paḍu,* to fall, with కొట్టు *koṭṭu,* to beat, means "to knock down." Thus: నేను అతని పడకొట్టినాను *nénu atani paḍakoṭṭinánu,* I knocked him down.

(x.) Paradigm of a Verb.

152. Having thus given examples of the verbs, both regular and auxiliary, it will be convenient to give an abbreviated form of a verb in all its principal moods, tenses, and

forms. The same word which has hitherto been used, is selected as an example.

Brief Form of a Complete Verb.

చెప్పు *cheppu,* to say.

AFFIRMATIVE FORM.

Present Participle.

చెప్పుతు *chepputu,* saying.

Past Participle.

చెప్పి *cheppi,* having said.

Relative Participles.

Present	చెప్పుతున్న	*chepputunna,*	that says.
Past	చెప్పిన	*cheppina,*	that said.
Aorist	చెప్పే	*cheppé,*	that says or said.

Verbal Nouns.

చెప్పడము	*cheppaḍamu,*	the saying.
చెప్పుట	*chepputa,*	
చెప్పేది	*cheppédi,*	

Present Indicative.

నేను చెప్పుతున్నాను *nénu chepputunnánu,* I say or will say.

Progressive Present.

నేను చెప్పుతూవున్నాను *nénu chepputú-unnánu,* I am saying.

Past Tense.

నేను చెప్పినాను *nénu cheppinánu,* I have said.

Past Imperfect.

నేను చెప్పుతూవుంటిని *nénu chepputú-unṭini,* I was saying.

Aorist.

నేను చెప్పుదును *nénu cheppudunu,* I said.

Pluperfect.

నేను చెప్పివున్నాను *nénu cheppi-unnánu,* I had said.

Progressive Future.

నేను చెప్పుతూవుందును *nénu chepputú-undunu,* I will be saying.

Perfect Future.

నేను చెప్పివుందును *nénu cheppi-undunu,* I will have said.

Imperative Mood.

చెప్పు *cheppu,* say thou.

Subjunctive Mood.

Present Tense.

నేను చెప్పితే *nénu cheppité,* if I say.

Pluperfect Tense.

నేను చెప్పివుంటే	*nénu cheppi-unṭé,*	if I had said.

Present Potential.

నేను చెప్పవచ్చును	*nénu cheppa-vatstsunu,*	I may say.
నేను చెప్పగలను	*nénu cheppa-galanu,*	I can say.
నేను చెప్పగలిగితిని	*nénu cheppa-galigitini,*	I should say.
నేను చెప్పతగినది	*nénu cheppa-taginadi,*	I ought to say.
నేను చెప్పవలెను	*nénu cheppa-valenu,*	I must say.
నేను చెప్పుదును	*nénu cheppudunu,*	I would say.

Past Tense.

నేను చెప్పివుందును	*nénu cheppi-undunu,*	I would have said.

NEGATIVE FORM.

Participles.

Present	చెప్పక	*cheppaka,*	without saying.
Relative	చెప్పని	*cheppani,*	that does not say.

Verbal Noun.

చెప్పకపోవడము	*cheppaka-póvaḍamu,*	the not saying.

PRESENT INDICATIVE.

నేను చెప్పను — *nénu cheppanu,* I do not or will not say.

PAST TENSE.

నేను చెప్పలేదు — *nénu cheppa-lédu,* I did not say.

PAST IMPERFECT.

నేను చెప్పడములేదు — *nénu chéppaḍamu lédu,* I was not saying.

IMPERATIVE MOOD.

చెప్పవద్దు — *cheppa-vaddu,* do not say.

SUBJUNCTIVE MOOD.

నేను చెప్పకపోతే — *nénu cheppaka-póté,* if I do not say.

PRESENT POTENTIAL.

నేను చెప్పలేను — *nénu cheppa-lénu,* I cannot say.

PAST TENSE.

నేను చెప్పలేకపోతిని — *nénu cheppa-léka-pótini,* I could not say.

PERFECT FUTURE.

నేను చెప్పివుండను — *nénu cheppi-unḍanu,* I will not have said.

PASSIVE VOICE.

చెప్పబడు *cheppabaḍu,* to be said.

CAUSAL VERB.

చెప్పించు *cheppintsu,* to cause to say.

REFLECTIVE VERB.

చెప్పుకొను *cheppukonu,* to say for oneself.

(8.) *ADVERBS.*

153. Adverbs of quality are, as a general rule, formed by adding కా *ká,* the infinitive of అవు *au,* to become, to nouns or adjectives, which, in composition, is changed into గా *gá.* Thus: త్వర *twara,* quick, త్వరగా *twaragá,* quickly; చల్ల *tsalla,* cold, చల్లగా *tsallagá,* coldly; సుఖము *sukhamu,* happiness, సుఖముగా *sukhamugá,* happily.

154. The English adverbs of time and place, such as now, then, here, there, &c., have inflexions, and are treated as nouns, receiving the addition of post-positions. Thus:

ఇప్పుడు *ippuḍu,* now, ఇప్పటి *ippaṭi,* ఇప్పటికి *ippaṭiki.*
అప్పుడు *appuḍu,* then, అప్పటి *appaṭi,* అప్పటికి *appaṭiki.*
ఇక్కడ *ikkaḍa,* here, ఇక్కడి *ikkaḍi,* ఇక్కడికి *ikkaḍiki.*
అక్కడ *akkaḍa,* there, అక్కడి *akkaḍi,* అక్కడికి *akkaḍiki.*
మొన్న *monna,* the day before yesterday, మొన్నటి *monnaṭi,* మొన్నటినుంచి *mounnaṭi - nunchi,* since the day before yesterday.

నిన్న *ninna,* yesterday, నిన్నటి *ninnaṭi,* నిన్నటినుంచి *ninnaṭi-nunchi,* since yesterday.

నేడు *néḍu,* to-day, నేటి *néṭí,* నేటినుంచి *néṭi-nunchi,* from to-day.

రేపు *répu,* to-morrow, రేపటి *répaṭi,* రేపటినుంచి *répaṭi-nunchi,* from to-morrow.

155. Some words which in English would be regarded as adverbs are, in Telugu, post-positions, and, as such are placed after nouns to modify or to govern them. Many of them are capable of receiving inflexions like nouns, and of being modified by other post-positions being affixed to them. Thus: మీద *mída,* above, the inflexion is మీది *mídi,* and మీదికి *mídiki* is 'upwards;' కింద *kinda,* below, the inflexion is కింది *kindi,* and కిందికి *kindiki* is 'downwards.'

156. Other English adverbs are contained in the structure of the Telugu verb; and, therefore, it is impossible to classify all the various kinds of adverbs with which English grammarians are familiar, in an Oriental language which is so entirely different in its construction. A few of the more common examples are given.

157. The past participle of verbs is sometimes used adverbially. Thus: తిరిగి *tirigi,* again, is the past participle of తిరుగు *tirugu,* to turn. In the same way, మళ్లి *maḷli,* again, is the past participle of మళ్లు *maḷlu,* to turn.

158. 'When' is rendered either by the subjunctive form, 'if,' or by the word అప్పుడు *appuḍu,* then, being

affixed to the indefinite verbal participle, the consonant ట *ṭa* being inserted. Thus: "when he comes" may be rendered either by అతడు వస్తే *ataḍu vasté*, or by అతడు వచ్చేటప్పుడు *ataḍu vechchéṭappuḍu.* In the past tense, "when he came," అప్పుడు *appuḍu* would be affixed to the past participle, and the sentence would run—వచ్చినప్పుడు *vachchinappuḍu.*

159. In a similar manner, 'while' is rendered by adding గా *gá* to the infinitive. Thus: అతడు వ్రాస్తూ వుండగా *ataḍu vrástú-unḍagá,* while he is writing.

(9.) *CONJUNCTIONS.*

160. Conjunctions are not used frequently in Telugu. The common English conjunction, 'and,' is not, as a rule, represented in Oriental languages; but the sense is carried on throughout a sentence where several actions are narrated, by the earlier verbs being placed in the participial form, and the sentence is concluded by the last verb being put in the proper mood, tense, and person agreeing with the nominative. Thus: I came and saw, would be rendered నేను వచ్చి చూచినాను *nénu vachchi tsúchinánu,* I, having come, saw.

161. When nouns are joined together, the syllables ని, న్ని, or నిన్ని *ni, nni,* or *ninni* are added to words ending in *i, í,* or *ai,* and ను, న్ను, or నున్ను *nu, nnu,* or *nunnu,* to words ending in other vowels. Thus: వానికిన్ని వీనికిన్ని *vánikinni*

vínikinni, to that man and to this; నేనున్ను నా స్నేహితుడున్ను *nénunnu ná snéhituḍunnu*, my friend and I.

162. యు *yu* is inserted before the final న్ను *nnu*, in the case of nominatives ending in *a* or *e*. Thus: మీరున్ను ఆయనయున్ను *mírunnu áyanayunnu*, you and he.

163. These conjunctions are, however, often omitted, or the final vowel is lengthened. Thus: అతడూ నేనూ *ataḍú nénú*, he and I.

164. The conjunctions 'either—or' are represented by the repetition of కాని *káni*, the negative relative participle of అవు *au*, to become, the కా *ká* being softened in composition into గా *gá*. Thus: మీరుగాని అతడుగాని వెళ్లవచ్చును *mírugáni ataḍugáni veḷla-vatstsunu*, either you or he may go. అయినా *ainá*, the affirmative relative participle of the same verb with the final vowel lengthened, is used in the same way. Thus: నేడయినా రేపయినా *nédainá, répainá*, either to-day or to-morrow.

165. If అయినా *ainá* is not repeated, it represents the adverbs 'even' and 'at least.' Thus: నీళ్లు అయినా యివ్వలేదు *níḷlu ainá ivvalédu*, they did not give (him) water even.

166. 'Neither—nor' are rendered by the conjunctions న్ని or న్ను, *nni* or *nnu*, with the negative verb. Thus: దీన్నిన్ని దాన్నిన్ని చేయకపోయెను *dínninni dánninni chéyaka póyenu*, he did neither one thing nor the other; *Lit.* he went without doing either this or that.

167. When కాని *káni* and అయితే *aité* are used with the negative verb in the final clause of a sentence, they represent the conjunction 'but.' Thus: నేను అతణ్ని పిలిచినానుగాని అతడు రాలేదు *nénu atanni pilichinánugáni atadu rálédu*, I called him, but he did not come.

(10.) *EMPHATIC AFFIXES.*

168. There are certain emphatic affixes in Telugu, which are in daily use. They sometimes merely impart emphasis to a word or sentence, and sometimes represent the English adverbs 'even,' 'very,' &c. They are expressed by the addition to words of the vowels *á*, *é*, and *ó*.

As a general rule, *á* represents interrogation; *é* emphasis; and *ó* doubt. Thus: వచ్చినాడు *vachchinádu*, he came; వచ్చినాడా *vachchinádá*, did he come? వచ్చినాడే *vachchinádé*, certainly he came; వచ్చినాడో *vachchinádó*, perhaps he came.

(11.) *INTERJECTIONS.*

169. The most common interjections are very short and simple words, as is the case in most languages. They express surprise or admiration, or are used to draw attention to any thing or person.

170. In calling a person or drawing his attention to anything, great care should be taken to use the appropriate particle, as the language requires as much discrimination on this point as in the judicious use of the pronouns.

Thus: ఓరి *óri,* ఓసి *ósi,* ఓయి *ói,* and ఓ *ó,* all represent, Oh! in addressing people; but the first should be used only in calling men of lower position than the speaker; the second in calling women of inferior rank; the third in calling men of equal rank; while the last is common to all. When using these interjections, the last syllable of nouns ending in *i,* should be lengthened, and the final syllable of other nouns changed into *á.* Thus: ఓ తండ్రీ *ó tanḍrí,* O father; ఓ రాముడా *ó Rámuḍá,* O Rámudu.

171. Plurals end in లారా *lárá.* Thus: ఓ తమ్ములారా *ó tammulárá,* O brothers.

172. అయ్యో *ayyó,* alas! and అయ్యయో *ayyayó,* alas, alas! represent grief; అబ్బా *abbá* and ఓహో *óhó,* astonishment; ఛీ or ఛీఛీ *chí* or *chíchí,* aversion or contempt; and భళీ *bhaḷí,* or భళా *bhaḷá,* praise or admiration. సద్దు *saddu* represents silence, hush!

173. ఇదుగో *idugó* and అదుగో *adugó,* lo here! lo there! are constantly used to draw attention to anything extraordinary that may be going on.

174. Certain words also are idiomatically used to indicate sorrow or praise. Thus పాపము *pápamu,* sin, and పుణ్యము *puṇyamu,* merit, are used in this sense. Thus: if something melancholy is mentioned, the exclamation అయ్యో పాపము *ayyó pápamu* would mean, 'O, how sad!'

IV. SYNTAX.

Nouns.

1. The nominative case in a sentence, if expressed, precedes the verb, as, రాముడు వెళ్లినాడు *Rámuḍu veḷḷináḍu,* Rámudu has gone.

2. In the case of pronouns, however, the nominative is generally omitted, the pronoun being really contained in the verb itself. Thus: యేమంటావు *yémanṭávu,* what do you say?

3. The verb agrees with the nominative case in number, gender, and person, as, అతడు వ్రాసినాడు *ataḍu vrásináḍu,* he has written: నీవు వ్రాసినావు *nívu vrásinávu,* you have written, &c.

4. An active verb governs the objective case, and the order in a simple narrative sentence is first the nominative, then the objective, and finally the verb. Thus: ఆ మనిషి అతణ్ని కొట్టినాడు *á manishi ataṇni koṭṭináḍu,* that man has beaten him.

5. In the case of nouns denoting inanimate things, the nominative is used instead of the objective, as, అతడు పండు తిన్నాడు *ataḍu panḍu tinnáḍu,* he ate the fruit.

6. Two or more nouns in the singular number joined by the usual conjunctions take a plural verb. Thus: రాముడున్ను భీముడున్ను ఊరికి వెళ్లినారు *Rámuḍunnu Bhímuḍunnu úriki veḷḷináru,* Rámudu and Bhímudu went to the village.

7. When the first and second personal pronouns are thus used, the verb will be in the first or second person plural, as the case may be. Thus: నేనున్ను నా బిడ్డలున్ను సుఖముగా వున్నాము *nénunnu ná biḍḍalunnu sukhamugá unnámu,* my children and I are happy.

8. When two nouns are joined together without a conjunction, the first is put in the singular, and the latter in the plural, number; as, అన్నదమ్ములు *anna-dammulu,* brothers; literally, the elder brother and the younger brothers; అక్క-చెల్లెండ్లు *akka-chellenḍlu,* sisters.

9. The inflexion is used to express the relation between two persons or things. Thus: నా తండ్రిగారి యిల్లు *ná tanḍri-gári illu,* my father's house.

10. The inflexion of nouns or pronouns with the addition of the third masculine personal pronoun, or with the addition of the pronominal fragments ది or వి, *di* or *vi,* the former for the feminine and neuter singular, and the latter for the neuter plural, denote close relation or possession. Thus: వాడు మావాడు *váḍu máváḍu,* he is ours; ఈ గుర్రము నా తండ్రిగారిది *í gurramu ná tanḍrigáridi,* this horse is my father's.

11. The doubling of a noun gives it a distributive sense, as, నెల నెల *nela nela,* every month, or month by month.

12. In nouns denoting inanimate things, the objective case is sometimes employed instead of a postposition being

affixed to the noun. Thus: వాడు నెత్తిని మూట పెట్టుకొన్నాడు *váḍu nettini múṭa peṭṭukonnáḍu,* he put the bundle on his head.

PRONOUNS.

13. When in English the verb 'to be' is used to indicate possession, the verb is omitted in Telugu, and the appropriate pronominal affix is added to the noun and combined with it, thus representing the idea intended. If the noun ends in *i*, the pronominal affixes in *i*, are used. Thus: నేను అతని తండ్రిని *nénu atani tanḍrini,* I am his father; నీవు అతని తండ్రివి *nívu atani tanḍrivi,* you are his father.

14. Other similar phrases are formed by using the pronominal terminations ను *nu,* వు *vu,* ము *mu,* and affixing them to nouns or pronouns, as the case may be. In nouns of more than two syllables ending in *u,* the *u* is changed into *a* before the affixed pronominal fragment. Thus: నేను అక్కడి కాపును *nénu akkaḍi kápunu,* I am a tenant there; నీవు ఎవ్వడవు *nívu yevvaḍavu,* who are you? నేను అతని మనమడను *nénu atani manamuḍanu,* I am his grandson.

15. The third person singular, and the second and third persons plural, however, remain unaltered. Thus: మీరు అతని మనములు *míru atani manamulu,* you are his grandsons.

16. The first person singular frequently has an entirely different form in conversation, the common objective case

being used; as, నేను అతని మనుమణ్ని nénu atani manamuṇni, I am his grandson.

17. The negative is expressed by the addition to the affirmative sentence of the negative form of అవు avu, to be, namely, కాను, కావు, kánu, kávu, &c. Thus: నేను అతని తండ్రిని కాను nénu atani tanḍrini kánu, I am not his father; నీవు అతని తండ్రివి కావు nívu atani tanḍrivi kávu, you are not his father; నేను యోగ్యుడను కాను nénu yógyuḍanu kánu, I am not worthy.

18. The reflective pronoun తాను tánu, which is very frequently used, is common to all genders. Thus: అతడు తన యింటికి వెళ్లినాడా atadu tana inṭiki veḷḷináḍá, has he gone home, or to his own house? తాను అక్కడ వున్నానని అన్నాడు tánu akkaḍa unnánnani annáḍu, he says he was there, literally, he says I myself was there.

19. A common phrase is formed by doubling this pronoun with the insertion of అంతట antaṭa, which is compounded of అంత anta, so much, and అట aṭa, they say, between the duplicated pronoun, the emphatic é being put as the termination of the latter. Thus: తనంతట తానే tanantaṭa táné by himself, or, of his own accord. Other pronouns are used in the same way, as, నాయంతట నేనే náyantaṭa néné, by myself.

20. The plural of తాను tánu is frequently used in token of respect, as, తమరు tamaru, your honour.

21. It may be useful to remark here that expressions which in English are rude and vulgar, are commonly employed in Telugu instead of the personal pronoun, and are not considered impolite or offensive. Thus: నా వొళ్లు కాకగా వున్నది *ná woḷlu kákagá unnadi,* I am hot, is literally, my body is hot; నా గొంతు కమ్ముకొన్నది *ná gontu kammukonnadi,* I am hoarse, or, my throat is hoarse.

22. As already stated in the chapter on Etymology, much care and tact are required in the use of the personal pronouns, when addressing people or when speaking of them; but a few additional remarks may not be out of place. The distinctions in etiquette are peculiarly minute, and demand much thoughtful discrimination. Consideration for the feelings of the people and knowledge of their character are necessary for the right understanding of these niceties, on which they lay great stress; and all who wish to become not only conversant with the language, but with the mode of thought and customs of the people, will take pains fully to understand those peculiarities of number and person and choice of pronoun, which tend to promote courteous and kindly conversation and address.

23. The singular number is generally used in addressing inferiors; but sometimes, as in the case of prayer or in referring to the Deity, or in speaking to very intimate acquaintances, relations, and friends, it is employed to denote reverence, love, and respect.

24. The plural should always be used in speaking of or addressing a person of high position or caste. Thus:

కూలివాడు *kúliváḍu* is a hired labourer, and తోటవాడు *tóṭaváḍu*, a gardener, both being of low station; but వారు or గారు, *váru* or *gáru*, should invariably be used when speaking of a man in the higher positions of life.

25. గారు *gáru* ought always to be placed after the proper names of persons of high caste or in good position, as, నెల్లూరి రామచెంద్రయ్య పంతులుగారు *Nellúri Rámachendrayya Pantulu Gáru*, where Nellúri is the family or surname, being generally the name of a village or a town, Rámachendrayya is the personal name, and Pantulu, the pandit, a title.

26. It is also inserted after certain nouns to indicate respect, as, నా తండ్రిగారు *ná tanḍrigáru*, my father.

27. ఆయన *áyana* and ఈయన *íyana*, the most respectful forms of the third personal pronoun, are followed by a plural verb. Thus: ఆయన నా దగ్గిరికి వచ్చినారు *áyana ná daggiriki vachchináru*, he came to me.

ADJECTIVES.

28. An adjective generally precedes the noun which it modifies, as, ఒక మంచిపండు *oka manchi panḍu*, a good fruit.

29. Adjectives are frequently placed before the personal pronouns, the initial vowel in అది *adi* and అవి *avi* being omitted for the sake of euphony, as, చిన్నవాడు *chinnaváḍu*, a young man; చిన్నది *chinnadi*, a young woman.

30. The force of an adjective is sometimes obtained by the combination of two nouns, the latter being influenced or modified by the former. Thus: దొంగ *donga* is a thief, and మాట *máṭa*, a word. When combined, దొంగమాట *donga-máṭa* means a falsehood.

31. Besides the mode of forming the English comparative and superlative by using only కన్న and కంటే, *kanna* and *kanṭé*, a periphrasis is often employed. Thus: అన్నిటి కంటే పొడుగుది *anniṭi kanṭé poḍugudi*, this is the longest, literally, if you speak of all, this is long.

32. Another periphrasis is formed by using the word చూస్తే *tsústé*, if you look. Thus: దాని చూస్తే యిది పొడుగుగా వున్నది *dáni tsústé idi poḍugugá unnadi*, this is longer than that, literally, if you look at that, this is long.

33. Another kind of periphrasis may be used, as, ఈ పది యిండ్లలో యేది మంచిది *í padi inḍlaló yédi manchidi*, which is the best of these ten houses? Literally, in these ten houses, which is good?

Postpositions.

34. An infinite variety of combinations can be made with nouns by the proper use of postpositions. A few observations, therefore, on the more important are needful.

35. The postposition యొక్క *yokka* is sometimes added to the inflexion of a noun to signify 'of;' but much more

frequently in books, and invariably in conversation, the inflexion only is employed. Thus: అతని పేరు *atani péru* and అతనియొక్క పేరు *atani yokka péru,* both mean 'his name;' but the former mode of expression is much more common.

36. The postposition కు or కి, *ku* or *ki,* has several significations, such as, to, for, in, at, by, according to the context in which it is used; but it has always the meaning of motion towards something underlying them all. Thus: ఇంటికి వెళ్లు *inṭiki veḷlu,* go home; మాటకు మాట *máṭaku máṭa,* word for word; రాత్రికి *rátriki,* at night.

37. As there is no verb to express possession in Telugu, the English verb 'to have' is rendered by a periphrasis, the postposition కు or కి, *ku* or *ki,* being used with the auxiliary verb వుండు *unḍu,* to be, either expressed or understood. As, రాజుకు నలుగురు కొమారులు ఉన్నారు *rázuku naluguru komárulu unnáru,* the king has four sons, literally, four sons are to the king; అతనికి నిండా రూకలు *ataniki ninḍá rúkalu,* he has much money, or, (there is) much money to him.

38. This postposition is used to express the distance between two places. Thus: విశాఖపట్నానికిన్ని చెన్నపట్నానికిన్ని యెంత దూరము *Viṣákhapaṭnánikinni Chennapaṭnánikinni yenta dúramu,* what is the distance between Vizagapatam and Madras? Literally, how far (is it) to Vizagapatam and to Madras?

39. It is also used to express relationship to a person, and to form degrees of comparison. Thus: అతడు నీకు యేమి కావలెను *ataḍu níku yémi kávalenu,* what relation is he to you? Literally, what must he be to you? దానికి యిది మంచిది *dániki idi manchidi,* this is better than that.

40. This postposition is used with nouns to denote time, as, కాస్త సేపటికి *kásta sépaṭiki,* in a short time.

41. The postpositions చేత *chéta,* and వల్ల *valla,* both mean 'by.' The former is really the original locative or instrumental case of చెయ్యి *cheyy,* the hand. It is joined to the inflexion of nouns, and its force will be best illustrated by the following sentences—ఆ పని నీచేత అవునా *á pani níchéta auná,* can you do that? Literally, will that work be by you? ఆ పని నాచేతకాదు *á pani náchéta kádu,* I cannot do it, literally, that work cannot be by me.

42. The latter is identical with an old Dravidian noun వల్ల *valla,* which is often used as an adjective, and it has very much the same meaning as చేత *chéta.* Thus: ఇది అత నివల్ల అయినది *idi atanivalla ainadi,* this was (done) by him; అతనివల్ల తెలిసినది *atanivalla telisinadi,* I learned it from him.

43. The postposition తో *tó* is the exact equivalent of the English 'with.' Thus: అతడు దాని కత్తితో కోసినాడు *ataḍu dáni kattitó kósináḍu,* he cut it with a knife.

44. The word కూడ *kúḍa,* commonly pronounced కూడా *kúḍá,* the infinitive of the verb కూడు *kúḍu,* to join, is fre-

quently added to తో *tó* with the purpose of making the sense of connexion stronger. Thus: అతణ్ని నాతోకూడా రమ్మను *atanni nátókúḍá rammanu,* tell him to come with me.

45. The postposition లో *ló* is affixed to the inflexion of nouns to denote the English prepositions in, on, among. Thus: అతడు ఆ పట్నములో కాపురమున్నాడు *ataḍu á paṭnamuló kápuram unnáḍu,* he lives in that town.

46. This postposition is often used in conjunction with other particles and postpositions to modify or alter the sense, but the meaning of 'in' always underlies it. Thus, the addition of నుంచి *nunchi,* from, gives the sense of 'from within,' 'out of;' as, అతడు పట్నములోనుంచి వచ్చినాడు *ataḍu paṭnamulónunchi vachchináḍu,* he came out of the town.

47. గా *gá* added to లో *ló* means 'within,' as, రెండు నెలలలోగా *renḍu nelalalógá,* within two months.

48. లోపల *lópala* also means 'within;' and, with an inflexion of its own లోపలి *lópali,* it means 'internal' or 'inward,' and this inflexion itself sometimes receives a postposition. Thus: లోపలికి ఔషధము యిచ్చినాడు *lópaliki aushadhamu ichchináḍu,* he gave (him) medicine (to take internally).

49. The most frequent combination of లో *ló,* however, is with the postposition కి *ki,* meaning, 'into,' as, నేను గదిలోకి వెళ్లినాను *nénu gadilóki veḷḷinánu,* I went into the room.

50. అందు *andu* is a postposition with very much the same meaning as లో *ló*; but, perhaps, not so strictly signifying 'within.' Thus: వనములో *vanamuló* and వనమునందు *vanamunandu,* both mean 'in the forest;' నీయందు నమ్మిక యుంచినాను *níyandu nammika yunchinánu,* I relied on you.

51. న *na* is affixed only to nouns ending in *u,* denoting inanimate things, and means in, on, or with, according to the context, as, చెట్టున *chettuna,* on a tree; వనమున *vanamuna,* in a forest; చెప్పున *cheppuna,* with a slipper.

52. The postpositions వద్ద *vadda* and దగ్గిర *daggira,* near, with the addition of కి *ki,* are used when motion towards persons or things that do not admit of entrance, is intended. Both of them have an inflexion which is employed, when the additional postposition is affixed. Thus: నీవద్దవున్నదా *nívadda unnadá,* have you got it? Literally, is it near or by you? రాజు వద్దికి వెళ్లినాను *rázu vaddiki vellinánu,* I went to the king.

53. Several pure Telugu words have a mode of forming an instrumental case peculiar to themselves. It would be an error to call this form irregular, because it is evidently one of the archaic methods of forming an instrumental ablative, prior to the importation of Sanskrit words into the language. Thus, from పల్లు *pallu,* a tooth, the instrumental form పంట *panta,* is derived, as పంట గొరికెను *panta*

gorikenu, he bit it with his tooth; from నోరు *nóru*, a mouth, నోట *nóṭa* is derived, as అతని నోట వింటిని *atani nóṭa vinṭini*, I heard from his own lips, or, at his mouth; from పేరు *péru*, a name, comes పేరట *péraṭa*, or పేర *péra*, as అతని పేరట ఉత్తరము వ్రాయించినాడు *atani péraṭa uttaramu vráyinchináḍu*, he wrote a letter to him, or in his name.

54. Many words, some of which are also used as adverbs, are affixed to nouns in a manner very similar to postpositions, such as, ప్రకారము *prakáramu*, according to, లాగు or లాగున, *lágu* or *láguna*, like, as, రీతిగా *rítigá*, as. Thus: ఆజ్ఞప్రకారము *ágnyaprakáramu*, according to orders; ఈలాగున *í láguna*, in this manner. Such words are often used after the relative participles of verbs. Thus: నేను వచ్చిన తరువాత *nénu vachchina taruváta*, after I have come.

VERBS.

55. The arrangement of sentences in Telugu, as in other Oriental languages, is the converse of that employed in the languages of Europe, and at first sight appears to be singularly inverted. The several clauses, however, run smoothly into each other, and are remarkably harmonious. Few conjunctions occur, and their place is supplied by a free use of participles and verbal nouns.

56. The verb is always placed last in a sentence, and the preceding clauses work up to it; permitting the meaning to culminate in the last word. Sometimes several participial clauses precede the final verb, which, in English,

would be rendered by clauses beginning with conjunctions. Thus: అతడు లేచి వెళ్లినాడు *atadu léchi veḷḷinádu,* he arose and went, literally, he, having arisen, went. The number of such participial clauses may be very considerable; but they all form a connected sentence, one gliding into another, until the sense is rounded off and completed in the final verb, on which the attention rests. The following sentence is given as an example:— ఒకనాడు మబ్బు గాలివాన పట్టి వాడ పగిలి చెక్కలు ఒడ్డుకు కొట్టుకొని వచ్చినవి *oka nádu mabbu gálivána paṭṭi, váḍa pagili, chekkalu oḍḍuku koṭṭukoni, vachchinavi,* one day a storm arose, the ship was wrecked, and the pieces dashed upon the shore.

57. Addresses and quotations are always put in the most direct form, the indirect form or *oratio obliqua,* so common in European languages, being never employed by Orientals. This adds vividness and picturesqueness to the narration. The speech or quotation, just as it was spoken or supposed to have been spoken, is generally placed at the beginning of the sentence, which is concluded by one of the following phrases—అని చెప్పెను, అనెను, or అని అనెను *ani cheppenu, anenu,* or *ani anenu,* all meaning, 'having said, he spoke,' or అని అడిగెను *ani aḍigenu,* he asked saying, or some similar phrase. Thus: నీవు యెవ్వడవని అడిగినారు *nívu yevvaḍavani aḍiginâru,* they asked him who he was, literally, they asked him, saying, who are you?

58. Sometimes, however, and especially when the speech to be narrated is long, it is preceded by a phrase corres-

ponding to our 'as follows,' such as ఈలాగు అనెను *ilágu anenu,* he spoke thus, or యేమంటే *yémanṭé,* if you ask what? with the words అని చెప్పెను *ani cheppenu,* or a similar phrase, placed at the end of the quotation or speech.

Verbal Nouns.

59. The use of verbal nouns, both as nouns and as a substitute for the direct tenses of the verb, is very frequent in Telugu. They are of three kinds, all having very much the same signification, namely, those ending in డము *ḍamu,* ట *ṭa,* and ఏది *édi.* The two former are subject to the same inflexions and variations as nouns of the class to which they correspond; and the third as the neuter pronoun అది *adi.* All take the usual postpositions. Thus: చెప్పడము *cheppaḍamu,* saying, corresponds with nouns ending in ము *mu,* being చెప్పడము *cheppaḍamu* in the inflexion, and చెప్పడమును *cheppaḍamunu* in the objective, and receiving postpositions, as చెప్పడమునకు, చెప్పడముచేత, *cheppaḍamunaku, cheppaḍamuchéta,* &c.

60. చెప్పుట *chepputa* corresponds with nouns ending in *a*; and చెప్పేది *cheppédi,* with the third neuter personal pronoun, becoming చెప్పేదాని *cheppédáni,* in the inflexion. The past relative participle with the pronominal fragment ది *di* affixed, can be manipulated in the same manner, namely, చెప్పినది *cheppinadi,* చెప్పినదాని *cheppinadáni.*

61. A few examples are given to illustrate the way in which these verbal nouns are made to serve as nouns or verbs. Thus: మీరు ఆ వుత్తరము వ్రాయడము మంచిదికాదు *míru á uttaramu vráyaḍamu manchidi kádu*, your writing that letter is not good. It will be observed that మీరు *míru* in the above sentence is in the nominative case governing the verbal noun, though in the translation the possessive pronoun is used. గుర్రము పంపడము లేదు *gurramu pampaḍamu lédu*, he will not send the horse, literally, the sending the horse is not.

62. The infinitive of a verb is, in English, frequently used as a nominative, the whole clause in which it occurs governing the succeeding verb; but, in Telugu, such a phrase would be converted into one ending in a verbal noun. Thus: మన రహస్యములను బయిట చెప్పడము అవివేకము *mana rahasyamulanu baiṭa cheppaḍamu avivékamu*, to tell our secrets is folly.

63. అతడు యిక్కడికి రావడానికి యేమి హేతువ *ataḍu ikkaḍiki rávaḍániki yémi hétuva*, what is the reason of his coming here? The foregoing sentence is an example of the verbal noun receiving a postposition.

64. The verbal noun is frequently used with the addition of parts of the auxiliary verb అవు *au*, to be; and is thus substituted for a verb. The present tense is used in all its persons in the following manner, అవుతున్నది *autunnadi*, being added to the verbal noun—నేను వ్రాయడము

వుతున్నది *nénu vráyaḍam autunnadi,* I write or I will write, నీవు వ్రాయడమవుతున్నది *nívu vráyaḍam autunnadi,* you will write, &c.

65. The past tense is used in a similar way, as, వ్రాయడమైనది *vráyaḍam ainadi,* I have written it, or, the writing is done.

66. The verbal noun in ట *ṭa* is used very much in the same manner as that in డము *ḍamu.* Thus: వారు అక్కడ వుండుట యెరిగెను *váru akkaḍa unḍuta yerigenu,* he knew they were there, or, he knew of their being there.

67. The following are examples of the use of the verbal noun in *édi*—వారు యిక వచ్చేది లేదు *váru ika vachchédi lédu,* they will not come again, that is, their coming again is not; అతడు వంటిగా వుండేది మంచిది కాదు *ataḍu vantigá unḍédi manchidi kádu,* it is not good for him to be alone.

68. The addition of the postposition కి or కు, *ki* or *ku,* to a verbal noun gives the sense of the English infinitive, as, అక్కడికి వెళ్లడానకు నాకు యిష్టము లేదు *akkaḍiki veḷlaḍánaku náku ishṭamu lédu,* I have no desire to go there, literally, there is not to me the desire for going there.

PARTICIPLES.

69. The participles of the Telugu verb are exceedingly useful, and, by their faculty of combining together the

different parts of a sentence, render the employment of conjunctions unnecessary.

70. The present participle is not in such frequent use as the past; but its services are chiefly available for the construction of some of the compound tenses of the verb. The final *u* is often lengthened, especially in composition.

71. As a participle is used to lead up to the final verb in a sentence, it is governed by the same nominative case, either expressed or understood, as the verb itself. When the subordinate action which is intended to be expressed by the participle or participles is simultaneous with that of the final verb, the present participle is employed; when it is antecedent to it, the past; and, when it is of a negative nature, the negative.

72. The following is an example of the use of the present participle:—ఆడుతూ పాడుతూ వచ్చినది *áḍutú páḍutú vachchinadi*, she came dancing and singing.

73. The past participle is very often used, and, as already stated, the sense of a sentence may be held in suspense for some time until several past participles have been employed, and then the verb completes the sentence. Thus: అతడు వెళ్లి చూచి తిరిగి వచ్చెను *ataḍu veḷli tsúchi tirigi vachchenu*, he went, saw it, and returned.

74. The repetition of a past participle signifies the repetition or frequency of an action. Thus: నడిచినడిచి నాకాళ్లు నొస్తున్నవి *naḍichi naḍichi ná káḷlu nostunnavi*, my legs ache

with constant walking, literally, having walked, having walked, my legs ache.

75. The negative participle is used in the same way as the other participles. Thus: వ్రాయకపోయిరి *vráyaka póyri,* they failed to write, literally, without writing, they went.

Relative Participles.

76. There is no relative pronoun in Telugu, because the force of the English relative pronoun is contained in the relative participles. A participle of this kind refers to the noun or pronoun which immediately follows it, unless it happens to stand between two nouns, in which case the relative force of the participle differs according to the case those nouns may be in. Thus: కాగుతున్నపాలు *kágutunna pálu,* boiling milk, the milk that is boiling; చంపినపులి *tsampina puli,* the tiger that killed; వ్రాసేవాడు *vrásé váḍu,* he who wrote.

77. If the relative participle of an active verb stands between two nouns in the nominative case, it is governed by the former of the two; but, if the first noun is in the objective it is governed by the participle, which, in this case, is governed by the noun that succeeds it. It is most necessary to bear this distinction in mind, as it influences the whole principle and power of the relative participle. This rule will be best illustrated by an example. Thus in the sentence అతడు చంపినపులి *ataḍu tsampina puli,* the tiger

which he killed, అతడు *ataḍu*, being in the nominative case, governs the relative participle చంపిన *tsampina*, which refers to the noun పులి *puli;* but in the slightly altered sentence అతణ్ని చంపినపులి *ataṇni tsampina puli*, అతని *ataṇni*, being in the objective case, the meaning is completely changed, and the translation becomes, 'the tiger which killed him.' Take another example. నేను పనిలో వుంచిన మనిషి *nénu paniló unchina manishi*, is, 'the man whom I employed,' literally, the man whom I put in the work, whereas నన్ను పనిలో వుంచిన మనిషి *nannu paniló unchina manishi*, means 'the man who employed me,' which is the very reverse.

78. If the relative participle is preceded by two nouns or pronouns, the first being in the nominative case and the second in the objective, and is followed by a noun, the latter signifies the place or the instrument, in which or by which an action was done. Thus: నేను పులిని చంపిన చోటు *nénu pulini tsampina tsóṭu*, the place in which I killed the tiger; నేను పులిని చంపిన కత్తి *nénu pulini tsampina katti*, the sword with which I killed the tiger.

79. The past relative participle is sometimes used in the sense of 'though,' without being connected with a noun; but, in this case, the final *a* is lengthened. Thus: నీవు వ్రాసినా *nívu vrásiná*, though you wrote; వారు యేమి చెప్పినా సరి *váru yémi cheppiná sari*, no matter what they say, literally, what though they say, it is well.

80. The relative participles are frequently utilized as indicating subordinate actions in a sentence by the addition of adverbs, postpositions, and particles. Thus, adverbs such as తరువాత *taruváta* and వెనక *venaka*, after, and ముందు *mundu*, before, are often affixed to the past relative participle, as అతడు వచ్చిన తరువాత *atadu vachchina taruváta*, after he came.

81. In like manner other adverbs, such as అందు *andu*, there, with the addition of postpositions, are often affixed to the participles. Thus: అట్లా వున్నందుకు *aṭlá unnanduku*, for its being so; అతడు అట్లా చేసినందుచేత *aṭadu aṭlá chésinanduchéta*, as he has done so; అతడు అట్లా చేసేటందుచేత *aṭadu aṭlá chéséṭanduchéta*, by his doing so.

82. The past relative participle is often used with the addition of the pronominal fragment of the third person to represent 'what,' or 'the thing which.' Thus: నాకు కావలసినది యిదేను *náku kávalasinadi idénu*, this is what I want.

83. The past relative participle is also employed with the help of certain adverbs, such as అప్పుడు *appuḍu*, then, and అప్పటికి *appaṭiki*, at that time, to signify the time of the performance of an action. Thus: అతడు వెళ్లినప్పుడు *ataḍu veḷlinappuḍu*, when he went; నీవు వచ్చినప్పుడు *nívu vachchinappuḍu*, when you came; యెంత వెతికినప్పటికిన్ని *yenta vetikinappaṭikinni*, notwithstanding the search made.

The Relative Aorist Participle.

84. The relative aorist participle is used in a similar manner to the other relative participles; but, as its name indicates, the sense is more indefinite than either. Thus: కొట్టేవాడు *koṭṭéváḍu* means he who beats, has beaten, or will beat, and the exact sense will be ascertained from the context in which the participle occurs.

85. It is frequently used to express habit, or custom, or continuous action. Thus: గంగవరమనేవూరు *Gangavaram ané úru*, the village called *Gangavaram*, which is the name it is always known by. నీవు చేసేపనులు మంచివికావు *nívu chésé panulu manchivi kávu*, the works you do are not good, that is, the deeds you are in the habit of doing.

86. Pronouns and pronominal fragments are often affixed to this participle, thus turning it into a kind of verbal noun, as, అతడు చెప్పేది వాస్తవము *ataḍu cheppédi vástavamu*, what he says is true.

87. Like the past relative participle, the aorist has often affixed to it adverbs or particles to signify the time of an action. Thus: నీవు వచ్చేటప్పుడు *nívu vachchéṭappuḍu*, when you come; నీవు వచ్చేటప్పటికి *nívu vachchéṭappaṭiki*, by the time you come; నీవు వచ్చేవరకు *nívu vachché varaku*, until you come. In the first two examples, ట *ṭa* is inserted by way of euphony between the final *é* of the participle, and the open *a* with which the affixes commence.

The Negative Participles.

88. The negative participles are used in a very similar manner to the positive, only in just the opposite sense. The negative participle is formed by adding క *ka* to the infinitive, as అట్లా చేయక *aṭlá chéyaka,* without doing so; రూకలు లేక *rúkalu léka,* for want of money; నిద్రచాలక *nidra tsúlaka,* for want of sleep; దోవ నడవక వున్నది *dóva naḍavaka unnadi,* the road is impassable, literally, the road is without walking.

89. The negative participle is idiomatically used in what, at first sight, appears to be exactly the contrary sense to that which is intended. Thus: అతడు రాక ముందు *ataḍu ráka mundu,* before he came, literally, before his not coming; అతడు చెప్పకముందర *ataḍu cheppaka mundara,* before he spoke, literally, before his not speaking.

90. Care should be taken to distinguish between the positive past relative participle and the negative, as they seem, at first sight, to be spelt and pronounced almost alike. Thus: పంపినందున *pampinanduna,* by sending, is formed by the addition of అందున *anduna,* to the past relative participle of పంపు *pampu,* and పంపనందున *pampananduna,* by not sending, is formed by the addition of the same postposition to the negative relative participle. It will assist the student in distinguishing between the positive and the negative to remember that the idea of negation in Telugu is

always expressed by the insertion of *a* between the root of a verb and the pronominal suffixes, a peculiarity which runs throughout the negative form of the verb.

91. The distinction between the positive and the negative relative participle is clearly brought out in the two phrases, నేను చేసినపని *nénu chésina pani*, the work that I did, and నేను చేయని పని *nénu chéyani pani*, the work that I did not do.

The Infinitive.

92. The infinitive is used directly, as in English, to signify the result of a certain action, and is governed by the verb which succeeds it, as, అతడు నన్ను కొట్ట వచ్చినాడు *atadu nannu kotta vachchinádu*, he came to strike me.

93. The particle గా *gá*, which is itself the infinitive of the verb అవును *aunu*, to become, the కా *ká* being changed into గా *gá*, when affixed to the infinitive of a verb, denotes time, and is usually rendered 'as,' 'when,' or 'while.' Thus: నేను చెప్పగా నీవు వినలేదా *nénu cheppagá nívu vinalédá*, did you not hear when I spoke?

94. It is frequently used with the infinitive of వుండు *undu*, to be, which is added to the present or past participles to indicate the time when an action is being, or has been, performed. Thus: నేను వ్రాస్తూవుండగా తొందర పెట్టవద్దు *nénu vrástú undagá tondara pettavaddu*, do not trouble me while I am writing; నీవు ఆ వూరికి వెళ్లి వుండగా వచ్చినాను *nívu á úriki*

veḷli unḍagá vachchinánu, I came when you had gone to that village.

95. When the emphatic affix *é*, with the insertion of *n* for the sake of euphony, is added to the గా *gá*, it is translated 'as soon as,' 'immediately,' 'directly,' the precise time of an action being indicated by it. Thus: మీరు వెలపటికి వెళ్లగానే అందరున్ను వెళ్లిపోయినారు *míru velapaṭiki veḷlagúné andarunnu veḷlipóynáru,* they all left directly you went out.

The Present Tense.

96. The present tense of an active verb expresses an action that is being done at the time of narration; and, when the present participle is used with an auxiliary verb, it signifies continuity of action. As, అతడు వ్రాస్తాడు *ataḍu vrástáḍu,* he writes; అతడు వ్రాస్తూ వున్నాడు *ataḍu vrástú unnáḍu,* he is writing.

97. It has also a future, as well as a present, signification, as వస్తాను *vastánu,* I will come, వెళ్లుతాను *veḷlutánu,* I will go.

The Past Tense.

98. But little need be said here regarding the past tense, as the sense of it is very much the same as in English. It is, however, sometimes used in a present sense, as, విన్నావా *vinnává,* do you hear? యేమి అన్నావు *yémi annávu,* what do you say? But, even in such sentences, a little careful observation will show that the sense is really

in the past tense, though the action has occurred just immediately before the question was put.

99. In the negative form this tense is often expressed by adding to the affirmative past the negative aorist of అవు *au,* to be. Thus: నేను వచ్చినాను కాను *nénu vachchinánu kánu,* I did not come.

The Aorist.

100. This is undoubtedly the most difficult tense to understand thoroughly, and to use accurately, because the sense frequently varies according to the context. It is in reality, as its name indicates, an indefinite tense. Thus, in the phrase, నేను యెరుగుదును *nénu yerugudunu,* I know, it has a present signification.

101. It is sometimes future, as, అతడు రేపు వచ్చును *atadu répu vatstsunu,* he will come to-morrow.

102. It often denotes doubt, as, అట్లా వుండును *atlá undunu,* it may be so.

The Impersonal Verb.

103. The impersonal form of the verb is very frequently used. Thus, instead of saying directly 'I know,' it is much more usual to say, నాకు తెలుస్తున్నది *náku telustunnadi,* it is known to me. The third person singular of the aorist, namely, తెలుసును *telusunu,* is common.

104. A very common impersonal phrase is కావలెను or కావలసినది, *kávalenu* or *kávalasinadi*, being the infinitive of అవు *au*, to be, with the addition of వలెను *valenu*, or వలసినది *valasinadi*, the third neuter singular of వలయు *valayu*, to wish. Thus: నీకు యేమి కావలెను *níku yémi kávalenu*, what do you want? Literally, what must there be for you? వచ్చు *vatstsu*, to come, is often used in this impersonal way. Thus: అతనికి తెలుగు వచ్చును *ataniki Telugu vatstsunu*, he understands Telugu, literally, Telugu has come to him. కలుగు *kalugu*, to be, is of frequent occurrence. As, నాకు న్యాయము కలిగినది *náku nyáyamu kaliginadi*, I have obtained justice, literally, justice has been, or existed, for me.

The Conditional or Subjunctive Mood.

105. The conditional or subjunctive mood is usually formed by affixing తే *té* to the past participle, and it is placed in a sentence before the final verb that governs it. As, అతడు వెళ్లితే నాతో చెప్పు *atadu vellité nátó cheppu*, tell me if he goes.

106. In the negative form, the negative participle is used with the addition of పోతే *pótě*, the conditional mood of పోవు *póvu*, to go, or of వుంటే *unṭé*, the conditional mood of వుండు *unḍu*, to be. Thus: అతడు రాకపోతే నాతో చెప్పు *atadu rákapóté nátó cheppu*, tell me if he does not come, literally, goes without coming.

107. Condition is also expressed by affixing అట్టయితే *aṭṭaité*, to the past relative participle, as, అతడు వచ్చినట్టయితే నాతో చెప్పు *atadu vachchinaṭṭaité nátó cheppu*, tell me if he has come.

108. The word పక్షమందు *pakshamandu*, that is, the word పక్షము *pakshamu*, side, with the postposition అందు *andu*, affixed, is added to the relative participles to denote supposition. Thus: అట్లా చెప్పే పక్షమందు *aṭlá cheppé pakshamandu*, if, or, in case, he says so. పక్షము *pakshamu* is a Sanskrit word, and, perhaps, the pure Telugu యెడల *yeḍala*, being the Dravidian locative plural of యెడ *yeḍa*, a place, is more frequently used, as, నేను అట్లా చేసేయెడల *nénu aṭlá chésé yeḍala*, on my doing so; అతడు నన్ను చూచిన యెడల *ataḍu nannu tsúchina yeḍala*, if, or, when he saw me.

109. When the action of a person is dependent on the course another pursues, and the sense of 'unless' is required, the emphatic particle *é* is affixed to the simple conditional mood, *n* being inserted for the sake of euphony, and గాని *gáni* is added. Thus: అతడు వస్తేనేగాని యీపని కానేరదు *ataḍu vasténégáni í pani kánéradu*, we cannot do this work unless he comes.

110. The conditional mood is sometimes used to express choice, as, వ్రాస్తేవ్రాయి *vrásté vráy*, write it, if you choose; చదివితే చదువు *tsadivité tsaduvu*, read it, if you like.

YES AND NO.

111. There is nothing exactly corresponding to these very common English words. The usual mode of answering a question is by repeating it, the termination of the reply being changed to represent affirmation or negation. A question is asked by changing the final syllable into *á*. Thus: అతడు నీ తమ్ముడా *atadu ní tummudá*, is he your brother? The correct reply in the affirmative is అతడు నా తమ్ముడు *atadu ná tammudu*, he is my brother, or by changing the final *u* into the emphatic *é*, అతడు నా తమ్ముడే *atadu ná tammudé*, certainly he is my brother; and the reply in the negative is అతడు నా తమ్ముడు కాడు *atadu ná tammudu kádu*, he is not my brother.

112. Sometimes అవును *aunu*, the third person singular aorist of అవు *au*, to be, is used to represent 'yes;' but it is not always the correct reply.

113. In the same way, if a verb is used, the question is repeated in the reply with the appropriate termination of the verb. Thus: వచ్చినాడా *vachchinádá*, has he come? the reply being either వచ్చినాడు *vachchinádu*, he has come, or రాలేదు *rálédu*, he has not come.

ON లేదు LÉDU AND కాదు KÁDU.

114. Clearness and facility of conversation very much depend on the careful distinction between the two common auxiliary verbs వుండు *undu*, to be, and అవు *au*, to become.

The two most frequently used parts of these verbs are లేదు *lédu,* the third person neuter singular aorist of the former, and కాదు *kádu,* the third person neuter singular aorist of the latter; and it is most necessary to bear in mind the distinction between these two very similar words.

115. In this grammar one simple rule regarding them will be sufficient. లేదు *lédu* always denies existence, being, or locality; కాదు *kádu* always denies essence, quality, or kind. In the two following sentences the sharp contrast between these two words comes out clearly—నా గుర్రములేదు *ná gurramu lédu,* my horse is not (there), నా గుర్రము కాదు *ná gurramu kádu,* it is not my horse.

116. The correct negative to an adjective is always కాదు *kádu,* as, ఆ పండు మంచిది కాదు *á paṇḍu manchidi kádu,* that is not a good fruit.

117. Other parts of these negative verbs have the same clear contrast. Thus: లేనివాడు *lénivádu* signifies, one who is absent, whereas కానివాడు *kánivádu,* one who is not on good terms with another. లేనివాడు *lénivádu* also means 'a poor man,' one to whom wealth is not. లేనిమాట *lénimáṭa* is 'a falsehood,' whereas కానిమాట *kánimáṭa* is 'an offensive word.'

Causal Verbs.

118. Causal verbs, which, as already stated, are formed by adding *intsu* or *pintsu* to the root of the verb that they

transform, govern the objective, or, in the case of neuter nouns, the nominative. They have a real causal meaning, that is, that one person orders or directs another to do something. Thus: ఇల్లు కట్టించినాను *illu kaṭṭinchinánu*, I built the house, literally, I caused the house to be built.

119. It should be observed that, in Telugu, distinction is always made between what is actually done by a person himself or by another at his command. Thus, in English 'I built the house,' may mean either 'I built it myself with my own hands,' or 'I caused it to be built by some one else,' but the distinction is carefully noted in Telugu.

120. The causal is sometimes preceded by the agent in the objective with the postposition చేత *chéta*, by. Thus: ఆ లెక్క తమ్మునిచేత వ్రాయించినాడు *á lekka tammunichéta vráyinchináḍu*, he got the account written by his brother.

121. Neuter verbs are frequently converted into active verbs by the causal form being used. Thus: పొంగు *pongu*, to bubble, is in the causal పొంగించు *pongintsu*, to cause to bubble or to boil, as పాలు పొంగించు *pálu pongintsu*, boil the milk.

122. Some pure Telugu neuter verbs have a distinct causal of their own. As,

కాగు *kágu*, to be heated, కాచు *kátsu*, to boil.

తెగు *tegu*, to break, *n* తెంచు *tentsu*, to break, *a.*

లేచు *létsu*, to rise, లేపు *lépu*, to raise.

వచ్చు	*vatstsu,*	to come,	రప్పించు	*rappintsu,*	to send for.
ఉండు	*undu,*	to be,	ఉంచు	*untsu,*	to place.
దిగు	*digu,*	to descend,	దించు	*dintsu,*	to lower.

Reflective Verbs.

123. As a rule, the addition of కొను *konu,* to buy, or to take, added to the root of any verb, gives it a purely reflective sense. Sometimes, however, it so completely alters the sense that it has to be translated into English by an entirely different word, although, if carefully examined, the changed word will be found to have a distinctly reflective meaning. Thus: మాట్లాడు *máṭláḍu* is 'to speak,' but మాట్లాడుకొను *máṭláḍukonu,* is 'to bargain for,' the meaning of which, being analysed, is really 'to speak for oneself;' అను *anu,* is 'to say,' but అనుకొను *anukonu* means 'to say to oneself,' 'to suppose,' 'to think;' నడుచు *naḍutsu* is 'to walk,' but నడుచుకొను *naḍutsukonu* is 'to behave.

124. The sense of reciprocity is sometimes conveyed by using the reflective form. Thus: ఒకరి నొకరు కొట్టుకొన్నారు *okari nokaru koṭṭukonnáru,* they fought together, or they struck one another.

Particles and Adverbs.

125. This abstract of the syntax will not be complete without a few observations on some of the more important particles and adverbs, and their position in ordinary sentences.

126. It has already been stated that the particle *á* is used to express interrogation. It is affixed at the end of the word which it is intended to modify, but it need not always be placed at the end of a sentence, being sometimes affixed only to the word which it emphasizes. The three following sentences are given by way of illustration— మీరు విశాఖపట్నం వెళ్లినారా *míru Vishákhapaṭnam veḷḷinárá,* did you go to Vizagapatam? మీరా విశాఖపట్నం వెళ్లినారు *mírá Vishákhapaṭnam veḷḷináru,* was it you that went to Vizagapatam? మీరు విశాఖపట్నానికా వెళ్లినారు *míru Vishákhapaṭnániká veḷḷináru,* was it to Vizagapatam you went?

127. The particle *é* affixed in the same manner to the last syllable of a word is the sign of strong emphasis, and must be translated by such words as 'very,' 'self,' &c. Thus: అతణ్ని ఆ దినమే చూచినాను *ataṇṇi á dinamé tsúchinánu,* I saw him that very day; మీరే రండి *míré raṇḍi,* come yourself; నేను రానే వస్తున్నాను *nénu ráné vastunnánu,* I will certainly come; అతడు రానేరాడు *ataḍu ráné ráḍu,* he will never come, or, he most certainly will not come.

128. By affixing the particle *ó* to a word, ignorance of a fact, hesitation, or doubt is expressed. Thus: అతడు యింట్లో ఉన్నాడో లేడో నాకు తెలియదు *ataḍu iṇṭló unnáḍó léḍó náku teliyadu,* I do not know whether he is in the house or not.

129. Sometimes a sentence begins with an interrogative pronoun or particle, and the sign of doubt or hesitation is

placed at the end of the first clause, a demonstrative particle or pronoun being used at the end of the sentence, which gives the sense of an English relative pronoun. Thus: యే కత్తితో ఆ పండు కోసినావో ఆకత్తి తే *yé kattitó á paṇḍu kósinávó á katti té*, bring the knife with which you cut that fruit, literally, with what knife you cut that fruit, that knife bring.

130. When యెవడు or యెవరు *yevaḍu* or *yevaru* is used in this way, the sense of 'which ever' or 'whosoever' is imparted, as, ఆ చిన్నవారిలో బాగా వ్రాసేవాడు యెవడో వాని పిలువు *á chinna variló bágá vrásévádu yevaḍó váni piluvu*, call the boy who is the best writer, literally, whichever of those boys is the good writer, call him.

131. There are really no adverbs in the Dravidian languages, but certain words have, from time immemorial, been used in the manner which would almost justify us in bestowing upon them that name. The infinitive of అవు *au*, to become, namely, కా *ká*, is one of these words. It is invariably changed into గా *gá*, and it has already been shown how it is used when joined to the infinitive of a verb.

132. It is also used after adjectives to convert them into what would, in English, be called adverbs, as, గాలి చల్లగా కొట్టుతున్నది *gáli tsallagá koṭṭutunnadi*, the breeze blows freshly; and it generally precedes the verb which it qualifies.

133. It is also used to denote quality, and is rendered by 'like' or 'as.' Thus: అది కొండగా అగపడుతున్నది *adi koṇḍagá agapaḍutunnadi*, that appears like a hill.

134. A very common and useful word is గదా *gadá*. It draws attention to a fact, the speaker expecting confirmation of or assent to his statement. Thus: వాడు దొంగ గదా నమ్మరాదు *váḍu donga gadá nammarádu*, surely he is a rogue, so you should not trust him.

135. Another word derived from అవు *au*, namely, కాక *káka*, with the addition sometimes of కుండ or కుండా *kunḍa* or *kunḍá*, is used to represent 'besides.' As, అతడు గాక నలుగురు వచ్చినారు *ataḍu gáka naluguru vachchinára*, four persons came besides him.

136. It is sometimes used after the aorist in an optative sense, as, నీ రాజ్యము వచ్చును గాక *ní rájyamu vatstsunu gáka*, thy kingdom come.

137. Another part of అవు *au*, namely, కాని or గాని *káni* or *gáni*, is frequently used as an adverb, or, more frequently, as a conjunction. Thus: నేను అతని చూడడానకు వెళ్లినాను గాని అతడు యింట్లో లేడు *nénu atani tsúḍaḍánaku veḷlinánu gáni ataḍu inṭló léḍu*, I went to see him, but he was not at home; యింతేగాని నేను యేమి యెరగను *intégáni nénu yémi yeragana*, I know nothing but this.

138. A common adverb, namely, మరి *mari,* is used to express 'more,' 'else,' and similar words. Thus: మరి వొకడు *mari vokaḍu,* another person. మరేమి లేదు *marémi lédu,* there is nothing else.

139. It is often used, with the addition of న్ని *nni,* at the beginning of a sentence in a narrative, and represents continuation, as మరిన్ని *marinni.* It may be translated 'moreover,' 'and,' 'and further.' When doubled, as మరీ మరీ *marí marí,* it means, 'more and more.'

We conclude this brief and simplified Grammar by giving a short piece of tolerably easy Telugu prose with translation and analysis.

THE ADOPTION OF A RAJAH'S SON.

అంతట బళ్లారి రామప్పనాయుడు చతురంగబల సమేతుడై వచ్చి, చిన్నవాడైన శిద్ద రామప్పనాయుణ్ని చూడగానే, యితడు తన పాదాలకు మ్రొక్కగా, లేవనెత్తి, ఆలింగనము చేసుకొని, గజారూఢుణ్ని చేసి, గ్రామ ములోకి తోడుకపోయి, సింహాసనముమీద కూర్చుండపెట్టి, తన జనులను పిలిపించి, ఆయనకు మ్రొక్కించి, నగరిలోకి వెంటబెట్టుకపోయి, లోగా వుండే అమ్మగారికి మ్రొక్కించి, బహు ప్రీతిగా వుండెను. యిక్కడినుంచి కూడపోయిన రాణువ సురికాండ్లకు జాతి ఆహారవస్త్రములు పంపించి, వారిని స్థలాంతరమందు దించెను. యీలాగున నాలుగు దినములు వారిని వుంచుకొని, అనంతపురం రామప్పనాయుని పేరట ఉత్తరము విశద ముగా వ్రాసి, క్షణేక్షణే అక్కడి వర్తమానము యిక్కడ, యిక్కడి వర్తమా నము అక్కడ తెలిసేలాగున ఉత్తరములు వ్రాసేటందుకు సెలవు యిచ్చి,

అంపించగా, రాణువవారు అనంతపురం చేరి, ఆ ఉత్తరము యివ్వగా, అనంతపురం రామప్పనాయుడు చూచుకొని సంతోషపడెను.

Then Ballári Rámappa Náyudu came forth accompanied by his army, and directly he saw the boy Shidda Rámappa Náyudu, the latter prostrated himself at his feet. Ballári Rámappa Náyudu then lifted him up; embraced him; seated him on his own elephant; brought him into the town; seated him on the throne; summoned all his retinue, and made them pay him homage; conducted him into his palace; made him pay his respects to his (adoptive) mother, who was within; and was exceedingly loving towards him. He then sent suitable food and raiment to the army and matchlock-men who had accompanied the boy from this, and caused them to encamp in a different locality.

He thus entertained the party several (that is, four) days. He then wrote a letter to Anantapuram Rámappa Náyudu, directed that letters should continually be written to inform each family of what was happening in the other, and sent them away. The whole party, on arrival at Anantapuram, delivered the letter, the perusal of which much gratified Anantapuram Rámappa Náyudu.—*Brown's Wars of the Rajahs*, III. § 25. p. 29.

ANALYSIS.

అంతట *antaṭa,* then. An adverb frequently used at the beginning of sentences and paragraphs, meaning 'afterwards,' 'then,' 'meanwhile.' బళ్లారి రామప్పనాయుడు *Baḷḷári*

Rámappa Náyuḍu, a proper name. Ballári, being the name of a well-known town, is the house or family name; Rámappa is the personal name; and Náyudu is the Rajah's title, which is usually borne by men of the Velama caste. This noun is the nominative case, and governs all the past participles in the sentence down to the final verb. చతురంగబల *chaturangabala,* inflexion of *chaturangabalamu,* an army, being compounded of the Sanskrit words *chatur,* four, *anga,* arms, and *balamu,* force, that is, an army composed of infantry, cavalry, elephants, and chariots. సమేతుడై *samétuḍai,* with or attended by. Compounded of the word సమేతుడు *samétuḍu,* a man attended or accompanied by, with the addition of అయి *ai,* having become, the past participle of అవు *au,* to become. A Sanskrit noun having been used, the Sanskrit equivalent for the simpler Telugu తోకూడ *tókúḍa,* is employed with it. వచ్చి *vacchi,* having come. The past participle of వచ్చు *vatstsu,* to come (iii. 126). చిన్నవాడైన *chinnaváḍaina,* who was the boy. Compounded of చిన్న *chinna,* small, వాడు *váḍu,* he, and అయిన *aina,* who was, or who had become, the past relative participle of అవు *au,* to become (iii. 53, 120). సిద్ధరామప్పనాయుణ్ని *Ṣidda Rámappa Náyuṇni,* a proper name, the title being put in the objective case, because it is governed by the following verb (iv. 4). చూడగానే *tsúḍagáné,* directly he saw. గా *gá* is here affixed to the infinitive of చూడు *tsúḍu,* to see, with the addition of the emphatic particle *é* and న *na* inserted for the sake of euphony (iv. 93, 127). ఇతడు *itaḍu*, he, the moderately respectful form of the third personal pronoun, referring to Ṣidda Rámappa, the boy who was about to be adopted. It is the nominative case governing the verb మ్రొక్కగా *mrokkagá* a little further on (iv. 3). తన *tana*, his. The inflexion of తాను *tánu*, the third personal pronoun, referring to Ballári Rámappa Náyudu, who was about to adopt him, and governed by the succeeding noun, (iii. 49). పాదాలకు *pádálaku*, at the feet. The second form of the inflexion plural of పాదము *pádamu*, a foot, a Sanskrit word, with the postposition కు *ku*, at or to, affixed (iii. 11, 26). మ్రొక్కగా *mrokkagá*, on bowing down or prostrating himself. గా *gá* is affixed to the infinitive of మ్రొక్కు *mrokku*, to prostrate oneself (iv. 93). లేవనెత్తి *lévanetti*, having raised. Compounded of లేవ *léva*, the infinitive of లేచు *létsu*, to cause to rise or to raise, and ఎత్తి *etti* the past participle of ఎత్తు *ettu*, to lift, the letter న *na* being inserted between the infinitive, and the open *e* of *etti* for the sake of euphony. The use of the double verb imparts to the former the meaning of 'up,' thus idiomatically avoiding the use of a preposition which, in many other languages, would be employed. ఆలింగనము చేసుకొని *álinganamu chésukoni*, having embraced him. ఆలింగనము *álinganamu*, an embrace, *S*. A neuter noun in the nominative case used for the objective (iv. 5). చేసుకొని *chésu-*

koni, having made for oneself. The past participle of the reflective form of చేయు *chéyu,* to make. (iii. 145). గజారూఢుణ్ని *gajárúḍhuṇṇi,* one that ascends (his) elephant. A Sanskrit phrase turned into a Telugu noun ending in *ḍu.* Compounded of గజము *gajamu,* an elephant, and ఆరూఢ *árúḍha,* ascended. Objective case governed by చేసి *chési,* having made, past part. of చేయు. గ్రామములోకి *grámamuló-ki,* into the village or town, *S.* The inflexion of a noun ending in *mu* with the double postposition లోకి *lóki,* into, affixed (iii. 10, 29). తోడక పోయి *toḍaka póy,* having taken him along with himself. A contracted form of తోడుకొనిపోయి *tóḍukonipóy,* having taken and having gone, తోడుకొని being the past participle reflective form of తోడు *tóḍu,* to take, and పోయి *póy,* the past participle of పోవు *póvu,* to go, here used as an auxiliary verb (iii. 127, 143). సింహాసనము మీద *simhásanamu mída,* on his throne. The inflexion of సింహాసనము *simhásanamu, S.,* with the postposition మీద *mída,* on, affixed, (iii. 10, 26). సింహాసనము is compounded of two Sanskrit words సింహము *simhamu,* a lion, and ఆసనము *ásanamu,* a seat, or a throne supported by sculptured lions. కూర్చుండపెట్టి *kúrtsunḍapeṭṭi,* having made him sit down. Compounded of the infinitive mood of కూర్చుండు *kúrtsunḍu,* to sit down, and the past participle of పెట్టు *peṭṭu,* to place. తన *tana,* his, the inflexion singular of the reflective pronoun తాను *túnu* (iii. 49). జనులను *janulanu,* people. The objective plural of the noun జనుడు *januḍu,* a man. *S.* (iii. 8.) పిలిపించి *pilipinchi,* having sent for or summoned. The past participle of పిలిపించు *pilipintsu,* the causal form of పిలుచు *pilutsu,* to call (iii. 149. iv. 118). ఆయనకు *áyanaku,* to him. The inflexion singular of the most respectful masculine personal pronoun with the postposition కు *ku,* to, affixed (iii. 48). మ్రొక్కించి *mrokkinchi,* having caused them to prostrate themselves. The past participle of the causal form of మ్రొక్కు *mrokku,* to prostrate (iii. 148, iv. 118). నగరిలోకి *nagarilóki,* into his palace. The inflexion singular of నగరు *nagaru,* a palace, with the double postposition లోకి affixed (iii. 15, 29). వెంట *venṭa,* with. Adverb. బెట్టుక పోయి *beṭṭukapóy,* having taken or conducted him. Compounded of పెట్టుక *peṭṭuka,* the initial పె *pe* being changed into బె *be,* a contracted form of పెట్టుకొని *peṭṭukoni,* the past participle of the reflective form of పెట్టు *peṭṭu,* to place, and the past participle of పోవు *póvu,* to go. లోగా *lógá,* within. Adverb. The adverbial sign being affixed to the postposition లో *ló* has the power of turning it into an adverb. వుండే *unḍé,* that was, the aorist relative participle of వుండు *unḍu,* to be, governed by the following noun (iii. 118, iv. 85). అమ్మగారికి *ammagáriki,* to his (adoptive) mother. The inflexion of అమ్మ *amma,* mother, with the addition of the honorific affix (iv. 25) and the postposition కి *ki.* మ్రొక్కించి *mrokkinchi,* having caused him to prostrate himself. బహు *bahu,* very. *S.* ప్రీతిగా *prítigá,* kindly. ప్రీతి *príti,* affection, love, kindness. *S.* A noun, with the adverbial affix గా *gá* (iii. 153, iv. 132). ఉండెను *uṇḍenu,* he was. The third person singular masculine of the past tense of ఉండు *uṇḍu,* to be (iii. 118). It may be remarked that, although it may be advisable to break up the above in translation, the one nominative case రామప్పనాయుడు governs every verb in this long sentence, with the single exception of the subordinate clause ending with the word మ్రొక్కగా *mrokkagá.* It governs ten participial clauses, concluding with the final verb ఉండెను *uṇḍenu* (iv. 56). ఇక్కడినుంచి *ikkaḍinunchi,* hence, from this place, meaning Anantapuram, where the writer was, and whence the adopted boy was brought. Thé inflexion of the adverb ఇక్కడ *ikkaḍa,* here, with the postposition నుంచి *nunchi,* from, affixed (iii. 154). కూడ *kúḍa,* together, along with. Adverb. (iv. 44). పోయిన *póyna,* that went. The past relative participle of పోవు *póvu,* governed by the following noun (iii. 127, iv. 77). రాణువ *ráṇuva,* the army. Noun in apposition with the following word. గురికాండ్లకు *gurikánḍlaku,* to the matchlock-men. The inflexion plural, with the postposition కు *ku* affixed, of గురికాడు *gurikáḍu,* a marksman, from గురి *guri,* a mark, and కాడు *káḍu,* the inferior pronominal masculine affix (iv. 24).

జాతి *játi*, caste, *S.*, according to the caste of each. ఆహార వస్త్రములు food and raiment, a common phrase, the Sanskrit form being used. ఆహారవస్త్రములు *ahára vastramulu*, food and raiment, *S.* The nominative plural for the objective of వస్త్రము *vastramu* (iii. 10, iv. 5). పంపించి *pampinchi*, having sent, or caused to be sent. The past participle of పంపించు *pampintsu*, a causal verb, to send. వారిని *várini*, them, the objective plural of వాడు *vádu*, he, governed by the verb దించెను (iii. 45). స్థలాంతరమందు *sthalántaramandu*, in another place, compounded of స్థలము *sthalamu*, a place, *S.*, the final *mu*, being omitted, and అంతరము *antaramu*, difference, *S.*, with the postposition అందు *andu*, in, affixed. The final *a* of the former word and the initial *a* of the latter are united by the Sanskrit rule of *Sandhi*, and together become *á*. దించెను *dinchenu*, he lodged them, or caused them to alight or encamp. The third person masculine singular past tense of దించు *dintsu*, to place or lodge, being the causal form of దిగు *digu*, to descend (iv. 122).

ఈలాగున *íláguna*, in this way, adverb, compounded of ఈ *í*, the demonstrative pronominal fragment (iii. 51), and లాగున *láguna*, like (iv. 54). నాలుగు *nálugu*, four. Four is here used as a round number meaning several days. దినములు *dinamulu*, days, the nominative plural of దినము

(iii. 10). వారిని *várini,* them (iii. 45). వుంచుకొని *untsukoni,* having kept, the past participle reflective form of వుంచు *untsu,* to place (iv. 122). అనంతపురము రామప్పనాయుని *Anantapuramu Rámappa Náyuni,* objective case. పేరట *pérata,* in the name of, being the original locative case of పేరు *péru,* a name (iii. 23; iv. 53). The Telugu idiom for writing a letter *to* a person. ఉత్తరము *uttaramu,* a letter, *S.* The nominative for the objective (iv. 5). విశదముగా *visadamugá,* clearly or particularly. A Sanskrit adjective turned into an adverb. వ్రాసి *vrási,* having written, the past participle of వ్రాయు *vráyu,* to write. క్షణే క్షణే *kshané kshané,* continually, from క్షణము *kshanamu,* a moment, *S.* The repetition of the words, with the addition of the emphatic particle *é,* represents continuity of action, 'moment by moment.' అక్కడి *akkadi,* the inflexion of the adverb అక్కడ *akkada,* there, governed by the following noun (iii. 154). వర్తమానము *vartamánamu,* news, *S.* Nom. sing. governed by the aorist part. తెలిసే *telisé.* యిక్కడ *ikkada,* here. Adverb. The next three words are the same as the preceding, the order being inverted. తెలిసేలాగున *teliséláguna,* so that it may be made known. The aorist participle from తెలియు *teliyu,* to make known, verb, governing both the preceding nouns, and modified by the adverb లాగున *láguna,* like, being affixed (iv. 88). The repetition of the phrase indicates the individuality of the meaning, "so that the news there may be made known here, and the news here may be made known there." ఉత్తరములు *uttaramulu*, letters. వ్రాసేటందుకు *vrásétanduku*, for writing. వ్రాసే *vrásé*, the aorist participle from వ్రాయు *vráyu*, to write, అందుకు, *anduku*, the adverb అందు *andu*, there, the postposition కు *ku* being affixed to it, and the letter ట *ta* being inserted for euphony (iv. 88). సెలవు *selavu*, order. The nominative used for the objective. యిచ్చి *ichchi*, having given. Past part. of యిచ్చు *itstsu*, to give. అంపించగా *ampintsagá*, on sending the people away. The inf. mood of అంపించు *ampintsu*, to cause to go, or to send. రాణువవారు *ránuvavúru*, the soldiers, governing the three succeeding verbs వచ్చి *vacchi*, చేరి *chéri*, and యివ్వగా *ivvagá*. అనంతపురము Anantapuram. To signify arrival at a place, the nominative is used as frequently as the inflexion with the postposition కు *ku*. చేరి *chéri*, having reached. v. n. past part. ఆ ఉత్తరము *á uttaramu*, that letter. యివ్వగా *ivvagá*, on giving. The inf. of యిచ్చు *itsu*, with గా *gá* (iii. 113, iv. 93). అనంతపురము రామప్పనాయుడు *Anantapuram Rámappa Náyudu*. చూచుకొని *tsútsukoni*, having seen for himself, or read to himself. The past part. reflective form of చూడు *tsúdu*, to see. సంతోషపడెను *santóshapadenu*, was gratified. Third sing. masc. past of సంతోషపడు *santóshapadu*, to be gratified, compounded of సంతోషము *santóshamu*, pleasure, *S.*, the final *mu* being dropped, and పడు *padu*, to suffer, which, being added to nouns, converts them into verbs.